TWO YELLOW SLICKERS

An Alzheimer's Memoir

BY

Phil Gilman McGourty

PSALM: FOR ALZHEIMER'S PATIENTS

(Gleaned from the Psalms and from Isaiah)

      "Come," I bleat, "come quickly now.

I am caught here in this thorn bush.

I can struggle no more.

My strength is gone."

The coyote crouches, readying to spring.

Now I hear my Shepherds steps,

He comes for me and my heart sings.

   I tell you all, sheep not yet born

Will hear me praise his saving grace.

His crook around my neck,

Leading me on his path.

Flinging wide the gates he showed me,

Green pastures, still waters,

Grain, laid out before me.

   I was in the deepest darkness then:

He came for me, and stood beside me.

His arm is now around me.

We shall always walk together

As long as my life lasts,

And after, when I see His Face.

This book is dedicated to my sister,
Sister Martha Ann Gilman, D.C., Ph.D.

My most loving and helpful support

And

To my daughter-in–law Michelle, who contributed
as my advisor, and also my friend.

P G McGourty

Prologue

Here, in this book, I tell about a physical and spiritual journey, taken with my husband as we walked with joy on green pastures, and then, carefully trod through the dark valleys of Alzheimer's.

I am convinced that the Supreme Being calls every person to experience his Presence, whether one calls him by the name of Adonai, Allah, Buddha, Brahma, God, the Highest Power, or any other name.

I have chosen Catholicism as my spiritual way because of the Sacrament of Eucharist. It is there, when receiving this sacred gift that I can contemplate the loving presence of the Good Shepherd.

As is true for all of us, I shall have to wait to see his face until I enter his Kingdom. May we all joyfully meet in that final, and eternal home!

P G McGourty

Book Chapters

CHAPTER ONE

Just Hold My Hand

I am not alone in my nostalgia for the past. From time to time we all look back in time to reminisce. Looking through all our photo albums that are tucked away in closets, and the individual photos that are crammed into boxes waiting for us to organize them, helps us to remember the past. The days and years of our lives are documented in each photo that is there. A photograph, however, cannot capture the emotions we had in the past like those feelings of anger and frustration that we felt at a certain moment, or the times when we were loving, kind, patient and tolerant of others. The attitudes that we expressed throughout our marriage and our parenting years as well as the intensity of our love for our spouse and for our children, the delight we experienced in the humorous episodes, and the sadness we endured in tragic moments cannot be preserved in a photograph.

Describing these emotions in writing can have a cathartic effect. I felt this healing as I was writing this book. Now I am hoping that this memoir will help others who are or have been the caregiver for a loved one who has now, or did in the past suffer with a terminal disease.

This memoir is the story of the journey taken with my husband through our married years and then continues through the fifteen years when my husband and I battled with Alzheimer's. Throughout all those years in the past we experienced many extraordinary joys and, alas, we also suffered a sad and challenging period when my husband was ill.

All through those later years we struggled to comprehend the meaning and purpose of suffering. Hopefully our efforts to understand these truths might support others who are faced with similar difficulties for we gradually did come to understand that whatever the meaning and reason for suffering, we would not have to travel alone when we were walking through this darkest of valleys.

There is no recovery from Alzheimer's. This illness generally progresses in a series of stages, usually termed early, middle and late Alzheimer's. For those under sixty years of age the stages move rapidly, lasting from three to five years. When it begins in later life it progresses much more slowly, lasting for ten years or more. My husband's illness lasted for fifteen years.

"However there are individual variations that can be attributed to numerous factors: the person's intelligence and abilities before his illness, his personality and basic ways of coping with problems, his marital relationship, and the degree of the environmental support that he receives." I am using this quote from Gruetzner* in order to explain with authority the validity that my husband was not a typical Alzheimer's patient and did in fact keep many of his mental skills until very late in his illness.

It is now time for me to introduce my husband and myself to my kind readers. My husband's name was Lawrence and mine is Philomene, but only Reverend Mother called me that, and then only when I was sent to see her because of some infraction of the school rules. All of my friends and my family call me Phil. My husband was called Larry.

In 1997 Larry was residing at the Brattleboro Retreat in Vermont in their brain disorder unit. He was in the fourteenth year of his illness. Before then he had lived with me in our home for thirteen years. Until the thirteenth year of his Alzheimer's he could enjoy conversing with others however, in the last years of his illness the facts he related were not always accurate. In his first year at the Retreat he would occasionally talk with Dr. Timothy Rowland, the Psychiatrist in charge of his care, about fly-fishing, a sport they both enjoyed.

In the years before he came to the retreat, when he was living at home he seemed to be stalled in the first stage of Alzheimer's with an occasional incident that definitely was typical of the middle stage. These incidents became much more serious in the last three years of his life.

Toward the end of 1997 when Larry first lived at the Retreat, I would visit him frequently. Whenever I visited him there our Toy Poodle Babette, and I would accompany him to the glassed-in porch at the end of the corridor. The patients were allowed to smoke cigars there when accompanied by a visitor. For as long as he enjoyed doing so I brought my husband a cigar to smoke. He would sit calmly smoking and I would join him in smoking my cigarettes. Between our conversations I would read to Larry from the Psalms. Sometimes I would read the Good Shepherd Psalm (PS # 23) as well as many others. Looking back to that time I hope that the Shepherd would have overlooked certain details as he watched us smoking and praying at the same time. Perhaps he watched with amusement and graciously excused these infractions.

After his admission to the hospital Larry was not, as I have said, a typical Alzheimer's patient. During his two-year stay at this facility, he was still able to speak and walk, and later in his second year there he still walked with the help of two aids. Even toward the end of his life he was aware of all that was changing in his mind and in his body and he was extremely confused and frustrated by his condition. On several occasions he expressed these feelings with anger, and, even at times, with rage. The staff of the unit where Larry was a patient was trained to handle these outbursts, sometimes having to restrain him, until the medication he was given calmed him. My husband was fortunate to be where he was because the staff always remembered to treat him with dignity, and to respect his personal "space," never neglecting to ask his permission to approach him in any way, even when it was time to give him his medications. He was never over-medicated, and, in his first year he walked unaided. At that time he was allowed to stroll the corridor at will.

One day, early in his first year at the Retreat, Dr. Timothy Rowland called me to explain that Larry had been moved to the diagnostic unit of the hospital in order to reassess his medications. To initiate this test all his current medications would have to be withheld from him. He was being watched carefully because it was certainly possible that he might now react to his illness with extreme violence. When I arrived that afternoon the person at the check-in desk advise me to sit in the hall until Larry's nurse came out to get me. Apparently he had had a very angry episode. Shortly after, I was escorted into my husband's room. I saw two well-muscled men standing at the head of his bed and two nurses standing near Dr. Rowland. On my way to visit my husband I had stopped off at the local Catholic Church to put a Host into my Pix so I could bring the Eucharist to him. Larry looked very angry when I reached his side. "Hello dear," I said nervously, "I have a surprise for you." "What is it" Larry replied, gruffly. "I have brought you Holy Communion," I answered.

"In that case." my husband said, "we should say a prayer before you give it to me." He folded his hands and, not waiting for others to join him, he began to pray. "Our Father, who art in heaven…." Without my prompting, he slowly and reverently recited the entire prayer by himself. Then he asked me to give him his communion wafer. After I had done this I looked around at all the staff standing beside his bed. Without exception each staff member had tears in their eyes and on their cheeks. As Dr. Rowland turned toward me his smile conveyed his amazement that the emergence of Larry's personhood should follow so shortly after a major angry, and apparently violent incident. It was indeed astonishing! However I had never doubted that Larry's mind was aware of the situation that he was in, and that his Alzheimer's had not deprived him of his awareness of himself or of the people around him.

Toward the end of his second year at the Retreat, as his illness progressed, he did enter into the last stage of Alzheimer's. At that time he failed rapidly becoming more fragile physically. Although he seemed to understand what was said to him at this time, he would answer only with a simple response. Yet, a week before he died, when being walked by his two hospital aids, one of them said, "You will be happy this afternoon for Phyllis is coming to see you." Quick as a snake attack, Larry reached out toward this aid and pushed her, angrily shoving her so hard that she fell to the floor. Clearly speaking, Larry said, "Not Phyllis! Her name is Philomene." With difficulty they quieted my husband. Even in these last days Larry knew my name and was concerned about me and understood my relationship to him.

Like the lady on his floor who used a wheeled walker, (and I will tell you about her later in this book) it seemed that he only spoke when he answered my questions or when it was important enough to matter to him to do so. Did this lady finally speak because she felt that our poodle Babette would listen to her? Apparently she felt that no one else would; that no one was interested in hearing what she had to say. If no one is willing to listen or to trying to communicate with you is there really any motivation to speak? What was this woman's experience before she came to the Retreat? She had been in this hospital for three years and had arrived there silent. For how long had she been silent before she came? And why? Had she been rejected? Had she felt lonely and abandoned? Did our little toy poodle's happy and approving spirit reach her inmost soul and fill her mind with trust, and with the courage to speak?

The nurses told me that the patients who had visitors were often easier to manage and help than those patients who had no visitors. Studies have shown that infants who do not feel loving touches and hear voices that murmur loving approval, suffer from what is called the "Failure to thrive" syndrome. This same situation applies to Alzheimer's patients.

This is a role that Hospice persons can provide. Even if verbal communication is no longer possible, the Hospice person can communicate love, acceptance and affirmation with touching and murmuring softly or speaking in gentle tones. In this way they can convey to the patient that they realize that their personhood is still present within them, and also convey that this hospice person wants them to know that they are not alone.

Doctor Rowland told me, the hardest thing for the staff in this facility to live with is the knowledge that these patients will never get better. If they have gotten to know the family of a patient, the staff will react to their death with even more sorrow and regret than they would ordinarily feel.

Shortly after the "name" episode Larry started to lose his ability to swallow, and was also no longer able to walk, even with his two aids supporting him. The head-nurse pointed out to me that the possibility of pneumonia or other infections was very real now, and the time had come for some medication issues to be addressed. I knew that I needed to consult with someone I trusted.

Over the months that Larry was in this facility Dr. Rowland had become a person whom I respected and trusted. When Larry had first arrived at the hospital this doctor had grown fond of Larry because they had fly-fishing in common. He and Larry would often talk about places to fish, and which were the best lures to use to entice a fish on to one's hook. I felt very comfortable consulting him, for he had honestly answered my questions in the past, and I had found his advice to be very helpful.

Once I confided in him that certain relatives were negatively critiquing the quality of care that I gave my husband while he was living at home, I had to bite my tongue, I told him, so as not to say anything scathing. His advice was, " You should have told them that you could have Larry packed and ready to go in ten minutes, for obviously he would get better care with them than with you. If you had said this they would not have troubled you anymore."

I was very relieved that this Doctor was willing to spend the time to discuss this troubling question of medications, and to offer his opinion to me. He gently explained to me that because Larry was nearing the end of this difficult and very long journey the administering of antibiotics, and certain medications, or procedures, might possibly result in prolonging or even increasing his suffering. "My advice" he said, "would be to request that your husband be given only medication that will lessen his pain and ease his anxiety". That seemed right to me. "However", he added, "to ensure this, even though you are the person holding his medical Power of Attorney, and a Guardianship, and had the foresight to have Larry sign his Living Will fifteen years ago you will still be required by the Laws of the State of Vermont to sign an order form requesting that this facility, and everyone on the staff here, be obligated to follow your wishes in this matter."

I felt my body shaking and tears filling my eyes. Although I knew that this must be done, I felt myself pulling back, unable to proceed. "No," I told him, "I could never do this."

"Do you understand why this is the right thing to do for your husband," he asked me. "Yes" I answered. "If I hold your hand," he said, "would it enable you to sign the appropriate form?" I looked up at him, unable to speak, and slowly nodded my head in agreement. "Come with me to the nurses' station" he said, "We will get the papers for you to sign."

We stood there, he with his hand over mine, as I signed where he indicated.

I could not speak or feel any emotions then. The tears still came, but my mind had completely shut the door to any thoughts about my husband's future.

Greutzner "Alzheimer's"

CHAPTER TWO

Shifting Sands

While sitting on the back patio of my son Eric's house his wife Jackie asked me, "How did you meet your husband and how did your life together begin?" I found myself laughing, and then to explain this unexpected response, I shared with her the story of how I met my husband Larry.

Like many well-meaning parents who are concerned about their children's future, two mothers conspire together and agree that it would be just delightful for one's son to meet the other's daughter. This must have been a feel-good moment for both of these women. Anticipating that this introduction might lead to a permanent arrangement, the first step of their hope-filled plan was put in place. I was that daughter and having no good reason not to, I agreed to their plans to go on a blind date with Thomas X.

Thomas X (I am kindly keeping his identity anonymous) was sent to pick me up at seven o'clock in the evening. I wore my blue taffeta dress, which was quite sophisticated, and had a rather low back. It seemed to me to be appropriate for an evening in Boston. At the time I was a junior at Manhattanville College that was then located in New York City. Thomas was in his senior year at Harvard. Because I had hoped for an evening of dinner and dancing at the Copley Plaza, in Boston, I was surprised when I saw Thomas turning the car away from Boston and toward the bridge that crossed the Charles River heading toward Cambridge. "Where are we going," I asked. "To Saint Benedict's Center, the Catholic Club at Harvard," he answered.

My mind was filled with foreboding. Having attended Newton Country Day School for twelve years, and now in a college taught by the same religious order, my definition of a date was anything other than a church related activity.

As the car made its slow way through the twisted streets and backed-up traffic in the city of Cambridge, Thomas recited a long monologue about how special he was. He was handsome he said, charming, intelligent and popular, the epitome of perfection, and a superb catch. This personal advertisement had continued through the entire drive east from the suburbs, like a variation on a musical theme. Never once did he inquire about my interests, hobbies, family, sports or any of the other usual conversation openers. Looking across at him, I had to agree that he was handsome; he had movie star good looks. It was also clear that Thomas expected total adoration from his dates. But after the one-hour drive to Harvard, I decided that Thomas's assessment of himself was way off the mark. I resolved to punish this boring egoistical date by shinning my charms on the first handsome man I saw when we arrived at the club.

I have been told that I was, in those days, a very beautiful woman. I had green eyes fringed with dark lashes, the same color as my hair. I was as intelligent as most of my friends, and I had inherited the subtleties of my father's dry Yankee humor. My comments often had a surprise double meaning, which people caught onto after a slight pause. In the Fourth Academic, which was my senior year at Newton I had been named the MVP for field hockey; this exercise had trimmed me down to a well-balanced five feet four inches. My father had said that all three of his girls were good-looking enough for all 'normal purposes'; this was his way of helping us realize that excellence of character trumps beauty. My sisters actually were both very intelligent and attractive women, each in their own way.

At last we arrived at the building where the Club met. I looked around the room and spotted my brother Jack Gilman chatting with a good-looking man in the back of the room. This man was tall, around six feet, with sandy hair and hazel eyes and the most amazing smile. "Okay, target number one spotted," I mused. As I walked over to join my brother and his friend I saw what I hoped was a look of interest in the young man's face as he extended his hand, saying, "Hello. I am Larry. And you are?" My brother Jack intervened, and said, this is my sister, Philomene". Larry knew Jack well. They were suite mates at Harvard and they often went out together to enjoy the myriad entertainments that Boston had to offer. I turned to include Thomas in this conversation but he had walked away to enjoy chatting with some of his friends who were there that evening. Not feeling neglected I continued to chat with Jack and Larry.

Larry certainly put "his best foot forward", and spent his energies charming me. We chatted up a storm that night. I learned that Larry's undergraduate education had been interrupted during the war when he had served as an officer in the Navy. I discovered that we both liked to read and enjoyed music. I loved opera and Bach; Larry loved the modern Russian composers, and especially Jazz New Orleans style. "Let's get together soon and spend an evening discussing books and music." Larry said. Something in the way he said this convinced me that he really wanted to do just this; this was not a "come up and see my etchings" invitation.

Later, as Thomas was driving me home he tried to charm me, and acted interested in me, but this attention was far too little and far too late for that. All I could think about was waiting and hoping for a phone call from this charming man named Larry.

What was it about this man that so intrigued me? Once home, and feeling a little bit like the heroine of a Victorian novel, I fell happily asleep in my cozy bed.

Larry did indeed call me, and often. Later, after I had returned to college, he frequently wrote letters to me, and I responded just as often. During the summer following my junior at Manhattanville we saw each other constantly and gradually fell in love with one another. That July, while Larry was serving his time in the Naval Reserve I met him at the Naval Officer's Club in Newport, Rhode Island, for a formal dinner dance. Larry looked especially handsome wearing his summer white uniform. Later that evening he escorted me out onto the terrace of the club, and, knelt down, asking me to marry him. The spring following my graduation from college we were married on April 15th, at St Vincent Farrar's Church in New York City, which was then my parents' parish church. Officiating was our dear family friend from Boston, The Most Reverend Bishop Eric F. Mackenzie.

I am told that it was a beautiful wedding, but I do not remember much about it. Now, when I look at our wedding album I realize that it was, indeed, an outstanding wedding. However, I had been so excited and anxious to begin our new life together with this remarkable man that I really have very little conscious memory of that day. After the wedding celebration ended and we had changed into our travel clothes and said our goodbyes, we began our drive south toward the first stop on our honeymoon at the Molly Pitcher Inn in Red Bank, New Jersey.

Despite Larry's many talents, he had never completed a driver's training program nor did he have a great deal of experience in city traffic enabling him to drive well. He drove for the first time during the war when a superior officer threw him a set of keys to a Navy truck and told him to report to the other end of the Island of Trinidad for an assignment. Larry's protest, "I do not know how to drive!" was answered by a curt, "You will by the time you get there." As a result the rules of the road were not foremost in his mind, although he did compensate for his lack of experience by concentrating on the traffic around him. At last we safely reached the Molly Pitcher Inn.

The next morning after a light breakfast, we continued on our way toward our next stop in Jamestown. As we traveled south on the coastal highway the traffic was light and the weather perfect. Suddenly a car passed us going far too fast and moving erratically, weaving across the road. As we watched, the car veered off the road, hit a raised collection of earth and rocks, and flew into the air, landing on its side on top of some small trees and shrubs. Larry, noticing that a man was caught between the front door of the car and its frame with the weight of the car door trapping him, said, "Phil, get out of the car and stand in the middle of the highway and try to stop a car to get help while I hold the door off that man. I do not think I can lift him out alone." So I got out of the car and finally was able to stop someone. Thankfully, this being the era before cell phones, the driver offered to go the nearest phone and notify the police. It seemed an eternity before the police car came to help us. Two policemen helped Larry lift the man up and out of the car and away from danger.

After the injured man was placed in an ambulance, the police turned to Larry and lectured him for his foolish, although well-intentioned effort to rescue someone. Did Larry not realize, they said, that the car could have caught on fire, or worse, it could have exploded with him standing on top of that car, which could have been a fatal bon-fire? If Larry had even the faintest hope of being recognized for his bravery, it evaporated in that moment. So much for the gospel parable of the man who had been robbed, beaten, and left bloodied lying on the side of the road. According to these wise West Virginia State Troopers, the Samaritan who sought to rescue the injured man, should have been aware that it might have been a set-up scenario, and fellow thieves might have been hiding, waiting to rob and kill anyone naïve enough to stop to offer help. Obviously Larry, this modern day Samaritan, should have sped on to the next town and reported this incident to the local police. Looking back on that day. I am proud of Larry's heroic actions but I am also grateful that he did not suffer any fatal injuries while placing himself in danger.

We finally arrived in Jamestown. While there, we bought a deep blue glass ornament that we later hung on our Christmas tree, for the art of glassmaking was one of the endeavors of the residents of that ill fated colony. Rising early the next day, we set off for our final destination.

At last we arrived in Georgia at the Inn on St. Simons Island. Gathering our things we walked into the hotel. Having stopped for supper on our way there, we opted, after checking in, to go directly to our room. It had been a very long day.

The next morning Larry gently shook me to awaken me, "Get up," he said, "the sun is up and so are the fish." I looked up at my new husband, standing beside my bed, dressed in his casual clothes, holding his fly rod, ready for a morning of fishing. "What time is it," I asked in a fuzzy voice. "It is 5:30 and the fish will be running," Larry answered. "5:30," I exclaimed. "You cannot be serious. This is our honeymoon, a vacation! On vacations ones sleeps late, eats, enjoys the beach and retires for a long nap, if you get my drift. After that, one showers and dresses for dinner, and hopefully with dancing." "I will meet you in the dining room at nine o'clock," Larry said, graciously accepting the inevitable.

This was a paradigm moment in our relationship. Larry would allow me to live my life on my terms as long as I offered him the same privileges. Thus began a long life of maintaining parallel lives, each supporting the other in our individual endeavors, and acting jointly on our common interests. We had begun a true partnership, each one of us gleaning strength and wisdom from the other. We were like a perfectly-matched pair of horses.

After breakfast, on that first morning on Saint Simons Island, we explored the common rooms on the first floor of the Inn and then decided to walk around this quaint town. We found the deli, and the bakery. There was a bulletin board in the center of Town Common displaying ads for several art galleries and postings for current events. There was no lack of things to do while we were there. We were charmed by this town and extended our walk to explore almost every street in the village.

Once we were back in our room we tested the comfort of our bed, which took quite a while. After showering we went out and tried our luck at one of the restaurants and enjoyed our first popovers, which were delicious.

The next day was even warmer then the day before; so we decided this would be the perfect day to explore nearby Jekyll Island. The manager of our Inn called the Inn on Jekyll and arranged for the rental of bicycles, and checked to make sure that the Innkeeper would pack a boxed lunch for us to enjoy on the beach. Before we left he gave us the schedule for the ferry.

I filled a beach bag with beach towels, sunscreen and what ever else I thought we might need while on the island. Wearing our bathing suits under our shorts and shirts, we set out for the ferry excited to be going to explore this famous island. When we got off the ferry in Jekyll we walked into the Inn and introduced ourselves to the manager. He gave us our lunch basket and showed us where the bicycles were kept. Then he gave us a map to guide us by the most interesting homes. "Most of the houses are boarded up now," he said, "but I have marked the ones where you can peek into the windows and get a feeling of how people lived here before the war. Actually they lived rather simply, considering the amount of wealth they had. Keep in mind that this entire island was private, owned exclusively by the occupants, thus ensuring that the owner's had total privacy from tourists. I have marked the best spot to enter the beach. So far you are the only visitors here today. I know that you will find this beach to be a paradise for you," he said smiling as he looked at our new and very shiny wedding rings.

We saddled up and began our bike tour of the island. The map the Innkeeper had given us was a great help. When we came near the houses that he had starred we would dismount and peek into every window. Having been given permission to do this, we took our time snooping. When we arrived at the beach entry we walked our bikes across the sands and left them at the foot of the first dune. Looking both ways, we saw nothing except the silvered sands and the dunes and the waves washing onto the shore which was covered with a variety of birds that were busy exploring up and down the beach. Larry pointed to where two large dunes formed a small cove-like area. "That might be a good place to lay out our towels," he said. "It looks as though those dunes will keep us out the wind, and it will be a cozy spot." As we were laying out our towels Larry said, "Let's try the water, and see if it is warm." So we removed our shoes, shorts, and shirts. Larry was laughing as he ran into the waves. I paused before entering the water. As I stood there the waves washed out the sand from under my feet. I shivered, because it was such an unsettling feeling as my feet sank farther and farther down into the sand. My grandmother who was fond of sayings, would have said, "Fear knocked at the door. Faith answered. No one was there." But at that moment I was troubled by this disconcerting feeling, as if I were standing in quicksand.

As I looked out to see Larry frolicking in the waves, those unsettling feelings washed away. I rushed out to join my husband in the sea. We did all the silly things that young people do: laughing as we splashed one another. Then Larry dove under me and lifted me high up on his shoulders. We played in the ocean until we were weary. "Let's lie on our towels and get a tan," I said. "Let's get a tan all over" Larry responded.

So we removed our bathing suites and stretched out on our towels. We were newly married and in love, new to each other's minds and bodies. One kiss led to another, and soon we were indulging in slow, sweet, and tender love.

Suddenly we heard male voices shouting and cheering, "Way to go" and "Go for it" and "All right" and "Good for you!" We looked in both directions along the enormous beach. No one was there. Then I looked up toward the sky, "Larry, look up!" I cried. Above us in the sky, not more than fifty feet away, was a navy dirigible, heading toward the mainland, its motor silent as it drifted slowly by. All the windows of the ship were crowded with sailors waving, as they applauded us and shouted their approval. Larry waved back, laughing and smiling at the sailors. I, also, waved back at them. But at that moment I paused, suddenly thinking, "What would Reverend Mother say to me now?" I decided that she would say, "Faith, hope, charity, and always remember that love is the greatest of these." I happily rejoined Larry in his laughter, and waved even more vigorously than before.

CHAPTER THREE

Green Pastures And Still Waters

Placing all our possessions in our new home in Vermont caused me to reminisce about other homes we had lived in and all the changes over the years that then enriched our lives. Especially important, and challenging, was the arrival of each of our four children. This experience defined our love in a new way. Now we had the responsibilities of parenthood with all its demands, its crisis to resolve, and its rewards to cherish. As the need for our love grew, so to did our partnership and our love and respect for one another. Of course we had predicaments and disputes to resolve as is true of any married couple with children who are at different stages of psychological growth. In this book I omit much of what happened over those years because any parent of four or more children could contribute their own happy or traumatic experiences; all those moments of their dealings with the ups and downs of parenting. These times contribute to and modify the kind of loving relationship a husband and a wife experience together; maturing it as well as strengthening it.

If the tapestry of our life were being woven over those years, the presence of our four uniquely different children, with their difficult and their triumphant moments would provide the saturated colors of the threads that would give this work much of its unique vibrancy.

Mother-hood exists in many forms. Biological mother-hood is perhaps the most intimate form of this relationship, step-mother-hood is certainly a challenging way to mother a child, and foster-motherhood, although temporary, is a supporting kind of motherhood and a unique gift to the child in care.

In our case we pursued adoption parenthood, another permanent form of this parent-child relationship. The commitment made on the part of the adopting parents to their adopted child is similar to a marriage vow; a promise made to be kept forever. This pledge will never alter, continuing with all their hearts, for the rest of this couple's life, for love once bestowed freely and completely has a life of its own. Although their 'parenting' role may in time eventually end, their 'loving' role does not.

I, for one did not choose to live in my children's pockets after they were married. My mother-in-law, the mother of five children, made it clear to me that she would baby-sit only in an emergency. Yet this woman became one of my best friends. I cultivated her friendship, welcoming her wisdom and appreciating her love for many years. When she died, just short of one hundred years old, I mourned her passing as my close friend, and as another mother.

On the days our children arrived Larry and I welcomed each of our children into our home and into the deepest recesses of both of our hearts. This is the place where each of them was truly "conceived". They were held close to our hearts from the time when we were told of their existence and 'birthed' at the moment when we first held them in our arms. Each day of our lives we have thought of them, rejoicing in their achievements and their choice of mates. We celebrated with them the birth of each of their children; our grandchildren, who now also continue to shower us with their gift of love. Our only regret was not having given biological birth to these children, for we would have no other but these children who are in and of our hearts. Our love for them had yearned for this reality.

Parents rejoice to see their children becoming independent and moving forward in their lives. Their only hope is that the children do comprehend, in their hearts, the enduring love for them that will always exist in the hearts of their Mother and Father. In our hearts we placed our constant petitions to the Presence, asking him to guard them, to guide them, and to enable them to move toward to the fullest completion of the personal and intellectual gifts that they have been given. This, of course is the prayer of any good parent, no matter the particular circumstances of their parenthood. In all these kinds of parent-hood none guarantees a perfect relationship.

Just as these children have weaknesses so too will those taking up the challenge of parenting. May the Good Shepherd teach us to see the blessings that forgiveness brings. Forgiveness for the child is a letting go of the wounds that the parents may unwittingly have caused, and forgiveness for the parents is a letting go of the wounds that the children may have unintentionally inflicted on them. Are any of us exempt from this need for forgiveness? Of course not! Yet the fullness of this grace rests upon those who choose to forgive, and the acceptance of this forgiveness clears the mind to completely rejoice in the love that is there in the other.

Looking back into the past I can see that our travels, our friendships and our children have enriched our lives. The quandaries and dilemmas we managed to resolve strengthened our characters, increased our mutual support of one another as a couple and as a family, and redefined our love for one another. Our marital and family partnerships are the constituent that determines the design of the final image of the "tapestry" that is to become the artistic portrayal of our lives.

I often think about our first home, which was west of Boston. In the fall, the foliage around our house would become brilliantly colored. In the spring the woods were lighted with the blossoms of the wild dogwoods and the mountain laurels.

We had been living there for several years before the day when we received a call from the adoption agency. Our new son would arrive in five days. Larry and I rushed into Boston to purchase a crib and all the other essentials needed for a baby. The store employees promised that everything would be deliver in three days. But then we received another call saying that the baby would arrive earlier on the next day. Luckily, Larry's brother Jack and his wife Mary had a new four-month-old baby. Mary said, "Yes, we can loan you diapers, bottles, and everything necessary except a crib." The result? The baby slept in a bureau drawer until his crib was delivered, much like a scene in the 'Little House on the Prairie!"

All through the months of waiting for our son to come to us I was nervous and concerned about the responsibilities of adopting. The enthusiasm and delight of my college classmate, Betty Reilly Steele was reassuring and comforting. Some of our older relatives could be seen frowning when the subject of adoption came into the conversation; some even tried to dissuade us. Betty's attitude toward our adoption of our first child was affirmative, and supportive. Sharing this experience with this kindhearted friend enhanced my joyous anticipation before our baby arrived and increased my elation when he finally did come. And when he did come he was so beautiful! Betty gave a copy of "Winnie the Pooh" to our son to "begin his Library", as she said. How fortunate I was to have her as my friend.

Three years later, my neighbor, Peggy Lannon, became a mother's "answer to prayer". Because I was a young and a relatively untried mother, she stepped in to support me when my sister Barbara Fagan became seriously ill, and my husband and I offered to take care of her three boys. Peggy loaned me four small iron cots that had been used for children in the cottage where her husband spent his summers as a child. When she arrived with these beds she explained that she had removed the round iron balls that topped the bedposts because she thought these four young boys, Larry age 3, Robert age 3, John age 4, and Ned age 5, might decide to play ball with them. Peggy's children were older than mine, and she knew a thing or two about young children. Everything went well for the first three days with Peggy coming each day, to help bathe and get the boys into pajamas and ready for bed.

On the fourth day Peggy said, "Phil, something smells odd. Let's walk through the rooms until we find where the smell is coming from." So we did this, and soon discovered that the smell emanated from the four iron beds. It seemed that all four boys had saved themselves a few trips to the bathroom and used the bedposts instead. Together, we removed the mattresses and bedding. Then Peggy called some neighbors, and soon four laughing men carefully carried the iron beds outside, turned them upside down, and, using the garden hose and liquid cleaner, cleaned them. Needless to say, Peggy became one of the friends whom I most admired.

Other than taking all four boys to the Doctor to have him remove Pussy Willows from all eight ears and all four noses, nothing serious happened while I cared for these boys. I never did thank the neighbor who gave me the Pussy Willows; it would have been difficult to be sincere in my thanks.

The boys stayed with us for eight weeks. One night, after they had all been put to bed, and I was thinking of reading my latest book, the oldest child, Ned, cried out "Auntie Phil, there's a lion on the drapery, and he is looking at me. Help!" I had never had to deal with a fear filled hallucination with my own son, so I was hesitant to help. Finally, I reflected," Ned believes the lion is real so I shall treat it as real." "Ned," I said, "I have a magic wand. It is very old and very special. I will get it. But before I do, everyone must be silent so as not to disturb the Lion". "Okay" Ned said, and the others agreed. So I went to the silver drawer and pulled out an antique letter opener. As I came back into the room I was chanting, and waving the "wand". "Lion, Lion, on the drapery. I am holding a magic wand. Listen to me. GO!" Almost immediately Ned said, "It's gone!" My special powers impressed them all.

The following May I was expecting a visit from a social worker from the adoption agency. We hoped to receive a second child. I had finished cleaning the house and then went outside to call young Larry to come in so I could dress him properly. Although he was not allowed to venture outside our back yard, he was nowhere to be found. I left a note and the door open for my visitor, and went out in search of my three-year old child. I found him, with a five-year-old neighbor, talking to two adults who lived on top of the high hill behind our house. The man explained to me that the boys had turned on his hose, placed it into his cellar window and flooded his basement. I started to apologize profusely, thinking, "There goes any hope for a second child." The neighbor interrupted my thoughts, saying, "Years ago, in the fall, when I was six years old, I turned on all the hoses in all the houses that I passed on my way to school. You can imagine how thrilled my parents were to receive numerous phone calls complaining about this situation. Boys will often find their way into problems such as this. So please do not be too concerned," he said, "Look at me, I grew up to become a minister."

When I arrived at home with my son Ms. Eileen Meany was waiting there. She looked at my three year old, standing in front of her, dripping water on the rug. "It looks like you had an adventure", she said to him. I explained what had happened and apologized for not being there to greet her. "Your son is more important than my visit," she said, "You did the right thing."

Two months later we welcomed a baby girl whom we named Maura, into our family. What a beautiful child she was! My son was happy to have a sister to boss around.

Three years later we welcomed our third child Eric. He too was such a handsome child. Now we had two boys and one girl. Young Larry had serious plans for his new brother. He was determined to turn him into an athlete. As soon as Eric was old enough he began an exercise program for him. This plan was successful for Eric did become a talented jock in high school.

Our daughter Maura kept praying for a sister. She must have had a direct line to God, for two summers later, we welcomed a tiny girl. The day the baby arrived Maura sat with her new sister Martha in her arms, her entire face lit with joy. "My very own sister" she said as she softly patted the baby's head. Now both sides were even, two boys, and two girls.

Martha often played with Tommy Sweeny when she was a toddler. Tommy's mother, Joan Sweeny is a dear friend of mine. Joan is erudite, humorous, and tolerant of my foibles. No wonder I love her! Many times Joan and her husband Tom helped us to box our possessions and then, after the move, unpack the contents, and put them away. They both exemplified the answer to the question, "What is a best friend like?" After they helped us handle our next move Joan told me that she was writing our information in her address book in pencil from now on because it was easier to change.

When Larry's commute to his office in western Massachusetts began to become too difficult, especially in the winter, we moved to a large house farther west in the state, closer to his work. This house was located in a very small town. It was built in1870, in the Carpenter Gothic style. This property had originally been a farm. It included a sizable spring-fed pond there, which my husband immediately stocked with several kinds of trout. We put a float out in the pond for the children to dive from in the summer. In the winter, when the pond froze, our boys, and their friends played ice hockey there, after they had cleared the pond of snow. Larry put lights into the trees around the pond so the boys could play in the early evenings. With visiting hockey players in winter, football friends in fall and baseball teammates in spring we soon learned the necessity of having a separate freezer with a lock on it. That way the expensive steaks were off limits, but the hamburger and fries were available.

Although the old barn that had been on the property was long gone, it did include a small stable where we could keep three horses, and the hay and feed they needed. There was enough land for the horses to graze on. We always had several Border Collies who delighted in chasing the geese that tried to swim in our pond. My daughter Martha would not be pleased if I did not mention that we always had several cats. Each one was uniquely different and all of them were especially fond of Martha.

This was the ideal location for our four children and their friends. This house became our most memorable home, the one that my children think of as the home that they grew up in. We lived there for eighteen years.

On one perfect summer day, when we were enjoying a barbeque with Joanne and Bill Wheeler, both Sweenys and six other friends, a car with New Jersey plates pulled into our drive. The driver leaned out of his car and asked," Is this a resort, and do you have a vacancy?" I was tempted to invite him in for a swim, but instead answered," We are full up for the week, sorry!"

One time as I pulled into our drive after a quick trip to replenish the pantry I saw Martha, age nine, sitting on the porch outside the kitchen door. "Hi Mom!" she said in an inordinately friendly voice. Had something happened? But, evidently not, for all seemed well. The next day, while getting the mail, I saw Bill Wheeler and he said," Quite a turn of events yesterday". "What events?" I asked. "Oh! Well, the cat's out of the bag now. Martha called me on the phone yesterday. Seems that Martha decided to surprise you and take the large tractor-mower and mow the lawn. Good plan, but the machine requires much more muscle than a nine year old child has. Thank goodness it did not tip over on her as she drove it into the pond. Big Pond, Deep Pond, Large Tractor! The moment I saw the problem I went home and got our farm tractor and pulled your machine out of the pond. Might be some water in the gas, but otherwise it doesn't seem that there are any other problems. And, Oh yes! I did give Martha a stern suggestion that she not drive this machine until she was at least sixteen years old."

The tractor incident was followed by my oldest son's moment to remember. When young Larry was in high school his knee was torn apart during a football game. We were fortunate to have a superb orthopedic doctor, Leo Buckley, who performed the surgery. The operation was challenging, and long, but all went well. Afterwards, my son had a cast on his leg from his hip to his foot. At that time Larry owned a large and beautifully trained seventeen-hands high horse of his own named Cinnamon. One day, only one week after his surgery, while I was out shopping for provisions, he decided to ride his horse bareback. The ride went without incident. If only he had kept this information to himself I would never have known that he had done this. After he returned to the house he decided to go up stairs to get something from his bedroom. This old house had a banister that would not pass the building codes today; it was very low because people were much smaller in the 19th century. To add to the difficulty the handrail was at least three times as large as they are now, which made it very difficult to grasp. As Larry descended the stairs, hopping on one foot, he could not use the rail to support and balance himself. He lost his grip and fell down the entire staircase, bumping his cast as he fell. It was amazing that he made his way back to the couch on his own for his cast was shattered. When I returned home I found him on the coach moaning, and in pain.

Needless to say my phone call to Dr. Leo Buckley did not endear us to him. I am sure that his wife, Pauline was not pleased that he had to rush in to the hospital. "There goes another day off," she must have said. Leo had to secure Larry's knee and replace his entire cast.

Who got the blame for this incident? The Mother! Yes, I did! Is it legal to chain one's adolescent child to a couch?

Unfortunately this accident ruined my son's football career. But he was still able to go fishing with his Dad. Larry took both his boys, Larry Jr. and Eric fishing every year. They went to a lake in New Hampshire and rented a cottage in a fishing resort. This was a bonding experience for the three of them. Both my sons still enjoy fishing, and have continued that annual family fishing trip together. Now the next generation joins them.

When the men went fishing every year the girls and I went exploring. We often went to the north shore, staying in an old Inn near to the shops and the art galleries, and of course, the beach. This area of Massachusetts includes some of the oldest towns in the Commonwealth. There was a beautiful old mansion nearby. One could tour the family rooms and wonder at their museum quality furnishings and art objects. We also could park and enjoy the beach that was covered with the softest white sands. Keeping up the quality of their tans was a high priority for these girls. Only as the sun was setting would they agree to leave and to return to our Inn for our evening meal. They announced this day to be the most perfect day of their special "all-girl" vacation. Although Maura and Martha were eight years apart they always enjoyed being with one another.

Larry and I enjoyed riding our horses over the miles of trails near our home. One time, after we had completed an especially long ride we stopped off at the home of our neighbor Harriet Goodwin to say a brief hello. Bantry, our Border Collie had accompanied us along the entire way, running circles around us, so he was truly exhausted. As we talked with Harriet he stretched out on the ground, panting. When we said goodbye and headed home we looked back to see that Bantry was standing beside Harriet's car. "Come with us" Larry called to him. But Bantry did not move. He just looked at Harriet and then at her automobile. "Oh all right", we could hear Harriet saying. "Let me get my keys and I will drive you home". She did just that. When she arrived at our house she let Bantry out of her car. Bantry looked at Harriet and then at my husband as if to say, "Some people understand the needs of a loyal dog."

For many years we celebrated the Easter holiday with our friends the Mehargs in our house with the pond, and with their children, Jodi and Maureen. We had gradually become close friends with this family during the ten years when we lived in Westchester County in New York. John was our pediatrician and his wife Nancy was my friend, we had much in common. These special friends were godparents to our daughter Martha, and Larry and I were godparents to their daughter Anne, who unfortunately died tragically when she was very young.

One Easter I decided to do a traditional Julia Childs' menu of roast suckling piglet. At least once in a lifetime I thought, we should enjoy this gourmet experience and have this classic dish. My butcher had prepared the roast for baking but had not removed the eyes. This chore fell upon John's shoulders for he was the closest in talent to an eye surgeon. I had the red cherries ready for John to place in the eye sockets and a polished Baldwin apple for him to place in its mouth. All six children from Larry Jr. age 18 to Martha age 8, clustered around John to watch this procedure. Jodi decided that the piglet should have a name. Many suggestions later they decided to call it "Flower". "What kind of flower?" Maureen asked. After much discussion they all agreed the piglet's name should be "Wild Flower."

Between the time that the roast went into the oven and the time that dinner was ready, in one voice all six children firmly declared, "We certainly will not eat "Wild Flower." Thus the children had their first vegetarian Easter dinner. This was not quite the palatial renaissance memory that I had planned for. I had to promise not to repeat this menu. I never did.

Before long our three oldest children were off to college, leaving only our youngest at home. When it was time for

Martha to leave for college I was bereft. The house seemed so empty. We no longer needed the extra freezer. We still had all our animals; so keeping them fed and happy was a grand distraction.

That was the year when I decided to learn to drive my newly purchased mare, Brivid's Burlesque, whom I called Gypsy. She had only been used for driving and had never been ridden, however I could handle the riding part, though teaching her that it was all right to canter while being ridden was a bit of a challenge. I did, however need lots of help in learning how to drive. After I bought a copy of an antique country cart for her to pull my friend Elsie Rodney, who was a professional trainer and instructor, taught me how to drive knowledgably and safely. Each time I was fitting the harness onto Gypsy and attaching the cart to her, my husband would stand in front of her to keep her still. Over time Gypsy seemed to trust Larry and always stood quietly for him. Gypsy also seemed to enjoy his company. In later years, despite Larry's Alzheimer's, this was a sport that he would be able to share with me. While I was fitting the harness to Gypsy and attaching the cart to her, Larry could 'head her up'. When we drove he could sit on the seat next to me and have all the fun of being in the competition. For many years Larry and I experienced this sport together.

Once we attended a Carriage Driving Competition at a lovely Country Club in Connecticut. We soon realized that the rivalry was fierce. We would be competing against several elegant pairs that were pulling handsome antique carriages. Gypsy however pulled a country cart, a Meadowbrook. This cart suited her for she was not a flashy Morgan but a strong, and willing old style Morgan. Because Gypsy was cautious, always carefully picking her way between the hazards, she did place many times in this class. Although she was slow she never knocked off the apples that were placed on top of the cones and therefore had no penalty points against her. However she did not place in that class at this show. Coming up two classes later was the Pleasure Class. I realized that we would not catch the eye of the judge with so many beautifully trained pairs for him to watch. The other horses represented the best of their breeds. Because we had come to this show to enjoy the sport and the camaraderie and not with expectations of winning, I decided to take Gypsy out to a field that was available nearby for anyone who was a contestant. I wanted Gypsy to relax and be ready to enjoy her next class, which was the Pleasure Class. We were only on the field for a few minutes when we heard loud honking from an unusually large flock of Canadian Geese. Within seconds we could tell that they were planning to land all around us. Gypsy began to shiver and gather her rear legs under her; a sure sign that she was planning to rise up and bolt. "You are all right Gypsy! Trust me!" I cried. She placed one ear back toward me but the other was facing the flock, as if to say, "easy for you to say. Those geese look like serious trouble to say." "Then Larry spoke to her in a soothing voice, "What a good girl you are! Such a good girl to stand and wait!! Very good to wait quietly." He continued to speak to her with these words and we could see that she wanted to please him for she had placed both her ears toward him so she could hear him over the racket the geese were making as they landed all around us. Gypsy continued to dance in place but she did not rise up in the traces or gallop hysterically away. This was truly remarkable! Men had come out to the field to help but as they watched they could tell that it seemed as though we had control of our horse. "Can we help?" someone asked, "No for she is obeying because she loves my husband and wants to please him." These men stood by, watching in amazement, as I finally asked Gypsy to do a slow walk. She obeyed and cautiously picked her way through the crowd of honking birds lifting and placing one nervous hoof after another until we were safely away from that large flock.

Now it was time for the pleasure class and Gypsy trotted happily in to join the other contestants. Considering her resent experience I was delighted that she was so calm and obviously enjoying herself. Finally the judge asked the class to line up. Gypsy did this perfectly. Now the judge left the ring and went back to the desk. Picking up a microphone he returned to the ring. This was most unusual, for the judge is never in the ring when the ribbons are called out. Then the judge began to speak reciting several of the rules that determine the winner of a pleasure class. "The horse must obey the whip no matter what the circumstances." Then he continued. "Today on these grounds we have witnessed a perfect illustration of the rules that I just read. There is a mare in this class who did not do what her nature told her to do, which was to take flight away from what must have seemed to her to be a dangerous situation. Instead this mare obeyed the whip and the passenger. Thus a tragedy was averted on these grounds." Then the judge approached Gypsy and said," This is why I am awarding Brivids' Burlesque the Blue Ribbon." He then pinned the ribbon onto Gypsy's bridle. And all the spectators clapped their approval.

Having Larry alongside of me that day was seriously providential, for he did indeed have a special relationship with this sweet mare.

Now that our children are grown and living independently, I am happy to report that they are all good citizens. They are very loving parents, excellent spouses, and kind to their aging mother. They have given me nine lovable grandchildren. Visiting these families is fun, and the food is top drawer. All of my girls are inventive cooks. What more can a mother and a mother-in-law want from her family? To be friends with my children, and my grandchildren, to enjoy occasional visits with them, and to eat well when I am with them. That is having the best of all worlds.

Larry and I loved to travel abroad and because of his business we had many opportunities to do just that. We were fortunate to become friends with Jiro Shigematsu, and his family, who lived in Tokyo, Japan. When she was a girl, Jiro's wife had attended a Sacred Heart School in China that was conducted by the same religious order that had founded the school that I attended in Newton, Massachusetts. This shared background gave us much in common.

One of my life's ambitions was fulfilled when Jiro arranged for us to visit the Buddhist Zen garden at Ryo-an-ji temple. He prearranged for a Zen nun to accompany us. I had studied Zen philosophy, Asian art and the Buddhist religion for several years at Boston University in their graduate school, having been accepted as a special student by the head of the philosophy department. Because of these studies I was thrilled that this woman would accompany us on our visit to this temple, for she was known to be an expert in these subjects. She would be qualified to answer any of my questions.

A Zen monk had created Ryo-an-ji garden centuries before our time. Today the design could easily be mistaken for a modern work of art. It was created to be a meditation garden just outside the Meditation Hall. Just sitting there on the steps of that hall, and immersing oneself in its multitudinous meanings, left one feeling, not puzzled, but ever so tranquil.

One evening, on this trip, we were invited to join several businessmen whom Jiro had invited to a special "Banquet" dinner. In the past Larry and I had met some of these men, and had even entertained some of them in our country home. One of these gentlemen had studied calligraphy for years and was considered an expert. He also had a deep understanding of Zen. He was the owner of several retail companies with which my husband had a business association. During the banquet this gentleman asked his guests to provide a response to a well-known Koan, which is a kind of Zen spiritual puzzle. After several guests had offered their answers, I decided to offer my version of one of the many classic answers. This upset our host. I was too late in realizing that he had been about to give us the answer. Obviously I had behaved like someone who told the punch line of a joke before the teller had the chance to do so. Our host turned to me and told me a Koan that stressed the importance of silence. Women in Japanese society are never invited to Banquets. As a visiting American woman they had made an exception for me. It was obvious that I had distressed this gentleman. Realizing my mistake, I sat through the remainder of the meal, feeling humiliated and embarrassed, with my eyes down, concentrating on my dinner plate. As we were leaving the party, one of this man's younger associates approached me and told me that our host hoped that I would agree to visit his home on the next afternoon to see his calligraphy. "Is this his way of forgiving me?" I asked. "He rarely invites visitors to his home," he replied.

His wife would be my hostess, as this businessman himself would be busy conferring with my husband. As we drove toward his home the young associate explained that he would act as an interpreter for me since the hostesses' English was iffy at best.

My hostess was an attractive woman. She was dressed in modern European dress, which surprised me. It was a large house, and extremely attractive. As we toured the house I noticed how beautifully arranged the flowers were, each in a perfectly appropriate container in a different Ikebana style. When I asked her about this she smiled such a happy smile and told me, in perfect English, that she had arranged them herself. She had studied this art for many years. I thought that her arrangements were some of the most beautiful that I had ever seen, and I told her this. As we sat enjoying our tea, I asked her how often she had a last minute American guest. She laughed and we shared the trials of being the wife of an executive. I then told her what had happened when we were entertaining six Japanese gentlemen at dinner at our home in Berlin.

We were starting to eat our main course, Filet Mignon, which was cooked medium rare. The evening was going swimmingly, (pun intended), when water started to pour down from the chandelier into the flower arrangement in the middle of the table. There was a stunned silence. Larry started laughing so hard that soon the others joined in. I rushed upstairs to discover that one of our kids had started to fill the bathtub, and then getting distracted obviously had forgotten to check the water level. Many bath towels later I rejoined the party. After one more round of scotch this incident became even more humorous to all of us. My hostess laughed heartily with a special glint in her eyes. I am sure, if she chose to, she could have responded with several stories of her own about entertaining American visitors.

As I was leaving this beautiful home to return to my hotel, my hostess and I, having discovered how much we had in common, kissed and hugged each other as we said goodbye.

Occasionally Larry and I would tack on a few days on to a trip and enjoy a mini vacation together. How fortunate that we had Marge Nowak to take care of our children when we were gone. One time, while away in Europe, we received a phone call from Marge. "I will not continue my stay here unless your children find a new home for the Boa Constrictor, Pinga, which I found in the game closet, on the second floor. Five feet of snake is more than I can handle."

I had no idea that we had a snake. A snake that was living in our house! I am terrified of snakes.

Larry then spoke to Maura, the child who owned the snake. It seems that somehow Pinga had escaped her cage in the basement and found her way up to the second floor while looking for a succulent mouse to eat. "You are to phone me in four hours reporting that Pinga, your snake, has a new permanent home," my husband said, and then added, "This is not a discussion. This is an order."

That snake lived in the Science Museum, in the city near us, for many years.

Our family survived many other adventures over these years. Too many stories to tell in this small book. Life certainly was never boring at our house.

CHAPTER FOUR

ONE THOUSAND MILES

I can finally remember what my husband was like before he had Alzheimer's. It took such a long time to let go of the recollections of those years when he was ill because of the gradual loss of his capabilities. His illness filled my mind like a spilled bottle of black ink, temporarily obliterating the recollections of happier days.

Today I look at those happy years separately from those sad years, almost as though they are the chronology of someone else's life. Unfortunately memories can be experienced as though they are current reality especially if the thoughts of the past only highlight the immense loss that lies in the present.

Remembering the past is like having one foot in a parallel universe. Much of what happened years ago undoubtedly affect aspects of our lives and personalities in the present day. From time to time our memories have a three dimensional quality with surround sound and saturated colors that vividly fill in the details of that moment. These are the déjà -vu moments that bring back to mind not only welcome memories of events of great joy, but also unbidden memories of intense sadness.

Now it is 2011 and it is spring here in New England, and my dwarf daffodils are blooming in my small garden. I have lived in Massachusetts for the past seven years. Some of my children live near-by. I love my condo; it is the sunniest home I have ever owned. There are times however when I miss my Florida condo, especially if the snow on my driveway can be measured in feet. In the spring I can look out my windows at the trees, the flowers and so many birds. I saw my first robin last week; she is back tending to her eggs in the nest that she rebuilds each spring under the deck of my porch. I can watch her when I am sitting inside my studio. This morning, as I sipped my coffee I watched a cardinal bathing in the birdbath. He was completely red with only a band of black to decorate his neck. He spent a full five minutes flicking his wings and his tail, concentrating on his bath. "You act as though you have an important date today" I whispered to him.

The sun rises outside my bedroom window and travels across the living room, dining room and kitchen window until it sets in the west thus filling my home with light all day long. While I am lying in my bed at night I can see the moon as it gradually fills itself until it becomes the perfect circle that is its completion.

I have placed some of our inherited furniture and Japanese prints in my living room. So many of our possessions evoke remembrances of our parents and grandparents and of exotic places where we have traveled. These treasures that Larry and I brought home from abroad compliment our family pieces. It is a happy setting for my present life. I am content here.

Today I bought some white Japanese Iris to plant in my new Zen garden. These Iris are very large and look quite a bit like Orchids. They will stand close to the dry pond and add brightness to this garden enhancing its Asian spirit. As I was positioning these new Iris, my thoughts wandered back to the time when my husband and I designed a Zen garden in our house in the country. Larry was still working then. We would sit there on the stone bench in that garden enjoying our cocktails while discussing all that had happened when he was traveling and at home while he was away. This was our private place where we could escape the cacophony of the children's voices.

I remember what a joy those years past were especially after he retired in 1982. His intelligence, his many years of reading on such a variety of subjects enriched our lives and also our travels at home and abroad. Our children were grown when he retired, and therefore we had the luxury of deciding how and when to spend our time. We were living the retired person's dream, enjoying each other's company, traveling together and often sharing our times at home with our good friends.

On one of our trips we were fortunate to travel to Nepal to visit Tiger Tops, riding on elephants to see the tigers there and the miniature Roe deer. On a trip to India, we stood in awe before the Taj Mahal, that magnificent testament to an abiding marital love affair. It was a special joy, at that time, to rediscover our mutual love and to be able to enrich our enjoyment of one another.

In those days we spent our summers up north in Bolton MA, and our winters on the gulf coast of Florida. When residing in Massachusetts, we attended art openings, and theatre in nearby cities and the musical events at Fruitland's in Harvard MA, where we would attend weekly Band Concerts with the audience sitting on the hillside overlooking the bandstand below. This was a natural amphitheatre. We always arrived early so we could secure a place on the level area on top of the hill. Once there we would claim a spot that gave us an unobstructed view of the bandstand below. We would shake out the newly washed horse sheets, set down the picnic containers on top of it and open our folding chairs. I would unpack the food and Larry would pour the chilled wine for our friends who had joined us for the concert. I would point out the level area in front of the bandstand at the base of the hill, "Just wait until you see the little children dancing to the music. They twirl and move about so charmingly. Later there will be another surprise, for the sun will set above the hills beyond. This is always a spectacular experience." As we listened to the music I thought of our past travels.

Over those years my husband and I had the pleasure of traveling on two guided trips abroad. We went to China with a small group lead by an expert American guide. Our first stop was the Forbidden City. We were fortunate to visit there for several days. The architecture and the amazing three-dimensional tile work that covered parts of the exterior walls were astonishing. The warm Chinese-reds in the tiles and the gilt details on the buildings gave the impression of nobility and power. One of my favorite memories while in China was of our trip by train to East Lake. There we visited an old

Buddhist Temple complex, which was covered with colorful tiles on the roofs that swooped up like the wings of giant birds. If you thought that Buddhism was a dour philosophy this temple was testament to the joyful manner in which its followers celebrated their spiritual journey through life.

In winter, after Larry retired, we were on the west coast of Florida in Placida. We often went to cocktail parties at our association and joined our neighbors at monthly dinner parties. Our condo was located south of Sarasota, which hosted an abundance of cultural offerings. With events at the opera, the theatre, the museums, and the horticultural association to attend, the choices for leisurely pastimes were innumerable. The restaurants in the area were superb and worth the hours drive. I joined the ladies book club that my friend Linda Smith organized. Our brains were being stimulated and our social life was first rate. This happy life lasted until the fall of 1984.

That summer time in Bolton had been busy and uneventful. Now summer in New England was over and the fall foliage that year seemed to celebrate the artistry of the forest, for the colors were at their most brilliant. However, the change of seasons that year seemed to me only to point to winter and frigid times to come.

Sadly and gradually, I had watched Larry's conduct change over a period of months. I noticed flashes of odd behavior, rather like things noticed peripherally when driving a car. It was like a lightening bug flying across one's path. Did you really see it? Like walking through a mist. Can you gather the moisture in your hands? Like gazing at the stars on a dark night. Did *you* see the falling star? I kept seeing hints of trouble. But the changes in behavior were so subtle it was hard to realize that they were significant.

Larry loved to walk down our long drive to take the mail out of the mailbox.

One day he came home without any mail so I started to go with him to get it. One week he paid the annual bill for his Wall Street Journal subscription three times, so I started to pay the bills. Having made a date with his mother he drove to see her in the same house where she had lived for years.

Later the phone rang. It was his Mother asking, "Is Larry still planning to visit today?"

The phone rang again. It was Larry calling, He said, "Phil, can you come and rescue me? I am lost."

When I added up all the things that were happening, I realized that something was clearly wrong with my husband. Perhaps he had had a mini stroke, I thought.

Our primary care doctor recommended a group of neurologists at a nearby hospital who were qualified to diagnose Larry. Having admitted to having a nagging feeling that something was wrong, Larry agreed to be tested. At the hospital they did several test including tests like cat scans and pet-scans. The names made me wonder whether we were in an animal hospital by mistake. The staff took a series of x-rays and did numerous other diagnostic tests. So many tubes were filled with Larry's blood that he asked the technician to leave enough blood for him to live on. They put suction cups on his chest and monitored his heart. At last the tests were finished. After we had lunched, we returned to the doctor's office. He reported, "I find no evidence of blood clots, strokes, cancer, heart problems, or any other significant disease. There is however one more test that I would like to do." "What kind," Larry asked. "Some verbal tests" the doctor replied. Larry was willing so the doctor began. "I am going to mention three words," the doctor said to Larry, "and I want you to remember them. I will ask you what the words are later in this test. These words are, a yellow rubber ducky, a book and an ice-cream cone." He then repeated these three words.

Next he asked, "Who is the head of government in Costa Rica and what is his title?" The Doctor asked at least five questions like that, all of them political. I was anxious because I did not know all of the answers.

Suddenly Larry stood up, reached for a sheet of paper on the doctor's desk, took it and covered up the doctor's question and answer sheet. "Doctor," he said, "can you answer these questions without looking up the answers on that sheet?"

I wanted to cheer, "Way to go Larry". I was so proud of him! To some of the other questions Larry answered, "My secretary always took care of that." Or, "I have never been interested in that subject", or, "That is why we have the Columbia Encyclopedia. " When it came time to tell the doctor the three words that were to be remembered I slouched lower in my chair for I could only remember two of them. Larry's answer was, "I only make an effort to remember important facts, and whatever those words were they will not change my day."`

Larry was taken to another room while I remained with the Doctor. "What, if anything, is wrong with Larry," I asked. "The doctor replied, "Your husband is not only an expert at covering up his disabilities, he also has a great sense of humor. However, I think he is in the very early stages of Alzheimer's.

I am going to give you the name of a doctor in Boston who specializes in brain disorders. I think that you should go to see him and get a second opinion. If he agrees with me then you can come back here to talk about the illness, the medications, and the care giving tasks, because this hospital is closer to your home."

I stood up and thanked the doctor; but my brain had not comprehended his diagnosis. On our way home I felt as though I were trying to find my way in the fog while driving over an unknown road.

The next day fall was at its most glorious. The sugar maple behind our house had turned a deep and brilliant crimson. Autumn was usually my favorite season. But this week I felt even more keenly that unusual sadness and alarming sense of loss.

The next day we drove to Boston for the second opinion. After a series of similar tests the doctor told Larry that his diagnosis was the same as that of the first doctor; Larry did indeed have Alzheimer's.

Larry and I made that long drive home in silence. I did not know what to say. Larry closed himself off from me sitting so still and never moving as he looked out his car-door window.

At dinner that night, Larry was clearly upset. He sat with his hands clasped as though in prayer, while his thumbs were constantly circling one another. This was something he did when he was upset and was concentrating on a problem he needed to solve. "Phil, I need to talk to you," he said sternly. "I do not have Alzheimer's. Something is wrong, but that is not what is wrong. I have worked hard my whole life. I have earned the right to live as I choose." Then his voice rose in volume, "Do you understand me?" He then paused to gather his thoughts between sentences. I did not dare to interrupt him during this stern speech. "I will drink wine if I choose to," he continued. (The doctor had said he should not imbibe alcohol.) "The house we live in is the house I have provided for you. Listen carefully Phil, I will not be legislated too." Larry's face had such a fierce look; I had never seen him like this before. Finally, I timidly asked him, "Do you plan to change your life in any way from now on Larry?" "I do not know," he answered. Then with the softest "Ah," he slowly got up from the table and left the room.

The house we were living in was next to a large tract of land that had been designated as state conservation land. Many wild animals lived there. We could occasionally see brown bears, deer, turkeys, and packs of coyotes: the coyotes apparently had taken up residence in the numerous caves that could be found on that land.

One afternoon we returned from shopping at the market to hear a pack of coyotes yowling on our back deck. They were chewing at the French doors that led into the kitchen. Our three border collies were inside the house. The female was in heat and apparently they were eager to reach her. Luckily, our garage had an entry to the kitchen. I closed the garage door and ran from the garage into the kitchen. I picked up the phone and called the police. They came quickly and shot bullets into the air, sending those eight animals running away in terror. We had to replace those doors because those coyotes had chewed them so badly. I began to wonder what would happen if Larry should decide to go for a walk in those woods alone. There was no way I could make sure that all the doors and all the grounds of that very large house were safe enough to prevent him from wandering into the woods around our house. I began to consider looking for a new residence where we would be within walking distance of a village with shops, and where I could secure the house and grounds.

While talking with my friend Harriet Goodwin, she mentioned seeing an ad for a house in Vermont, in a village near her home. This house had a five-foot high fenced in back yard. I had not considered moving out of state, but nevertheless, I decided to drive up north and see this house. I fell in love with it. The house was built in 1840. It was a brick house, a modified cape. I could lock both front doors with keys and still leave the back door open to the fenced in area that included a large patio covered with flagstones. Larry would be free to go out to sit there anytime he wished. We could also use this exit as an emergency exit, if it became necessary.

After much soul-searching I decided to buy this house and move to this village. I know some of my friends considered this move to be a geographic cure, a way of running away from the reality of Larry's illness. What ever my subconscious reasons, this move proved to be fortuitous.

Before we moved I went to a bookstore and bought a number of books on Alzheimer's. The more I read about this illness, the more this new information disturbed and overwhelmed me. It seemed to me that it would be impossible to deal with this illness on my own. I was frightened. I felt totally desperate and helpless. Although Larry had been angry when we talked, I did not think that his anger had been directed at me, but rather against the frustration he felt because of this diagnosis. Certainly he realized he would be facing the beginning of a fatal progression. Where and how would we find the strength to begin this new life together?

It seemed to me that this reality was carved in stone. No counseling or any amount of money could change this reality or the eventual outcome of this disastrous prognosis. Our family and friends could do nothing to alter this inevitability.

The next morning, as I was making our coffee, (my friends said that one could skate on my coffee.) I began again to mull over the options available to me. I understood that I would need a lawyer, a financial advisor, and our insurance man. Of course I did. Yet these were only practical steps, not tools that would enable me to make the right decisions, and to act in the most supportive way for Larry in future years. I realized that my German genes were checking in, making me feel that I should be able to control this situation all by myself. However, my English and Irish genes reminded me I really could not change this eventuality, and the future that this diagnosis foretold. I remembered that Larry always advised his children that the way to survive life's vicissitudes was to change your perspective on the problem. "Consider changing your attitude," he would say. "Seek the best and most practical solution and then move on. Accept what ever troubles remain; those are things which you could not change." I understood that I would have to find ways to change my response to this distressing news. I thought of praying for God's help. I wasn't sure how God fit into this dilemma, but I was convinced that without his willingness to intervene so I could achieve a modicum of success on this journey, I would be totally powerless to deal effectively with Larry's Alzheimer's and to survive it's effects on my own life.

I sat for a long time, sipping my coffee, and thinking, "What do I require most from God," I wondered, presuming that he was willing to give me what I asked for? If this journey was his will for Larry and me, I did not need to understand it so much as that I needed to accept this reality. I would need enormous trust and also God's constant help in order to survive with my mind intact for I did not know how many years I would need to endure and survive what could end up being a very long journey.

Then I remembered a period, years before, when one of our children had slid into a self-destructive way of life. I did not know what more I could do for this child. In desperation, I took this child's picture and put it behind a small wood-block print that was created by Albrecht Durer that depicts Christ's resurrection from the dead. At that time I thought, surely Christ would care for this lost sheep and save this child. Then I prayed, "Dear Shepherd, nothing I have done for this child has made a difference in my child's behavior. Will you intervene in this young life? If I turn this child's welfare and all my concerns over to you, will you lead my child on the right path?" Remembering these moments helped me to realize what I needed to request of God, for he had answered my prayers those many years ago. I would admit to him that I felt powerless to undertake this responsibility for my husband. I would ask him for his support in turning my will over to his. I would ask him to help me accept what was to come. I would ask him to stay near my husband and me to comfort us, and to guide us, for I knew I could not do this alone.

Suddenly I felt liberated. This awesome task that faced me was not mine alone. This insight was like the Zen Master's advice to leap off the cliff into the unknown, a courageous act, but a freeing action. I was relieved, realizing how much easier this journey would be with the Good Shepherd as our support system.

Yes, I was faulted, but we are all faulted and need one another's acceptance. We are not isolated from one another. Each of us needs tolerance, forgiveness, love and support from one another. This, of course, was exactly the kind of help I was asking from God.

From that time on I called God the "Presence." For, when Moses asked God what his name was, he said, "I am who am." He was the essence of 'BEING', an intelligence presence to Moses, expressing his loving concern for his people. I decided to relate to this Presence as one does with friends. Friends keep in touch with one another by writing, calling or texting them, so I determined to let the Presence into my life by chatting with him frequently in order to strengthen my friendship with him, and, I naïvely thought, to assure an increase of his awareness of me.

You, gentle reader, should know that I feel extremely brave in opening up my soul to you in this way. I am by nature, a private person, but I have been open and honest with you while writing this book, because as I look back over these years of caring, I realize that I could never have done it all alone. I needed the power of the Presence beside me in order to continue on this long journey. I want others to know that they also do not need to walk alone along any rocky paths; this is my purpose for writing this book and sharing everything that is in my heart.

Shortly after this day, I hired a consulting group that specialized in advising families about how to deal with the ramifications of Alzheimer's. The group advised our children to participate in the care of their father, and to spend time with him. By sharing these duties they would be able to relieve me as primary care giver and stagger these responsibilities. The representatives gave us literature on how to choose respite care or a nursing home. They recommended that I talk to my insurance and Medicare representatives to find out which services were available to us. They gave us a printed list of possible reactions and behaviors of the patient as the illness progressed. They also gave us a list of three books to read. Most, if not all of their advice came from one of the books that I had previously bought. "The 36 Hour Day." I could have saved a considerable consulting fee if I had just relied on this book's advice. (Recently I re-read this book and I still think that it is still one of the best books for caregivers.) The result of this costly consultation was that nothing dramatically changed because we had not set a plan in place that was carved in stone.

I find it fascinating how alike these issues are the world over. One of my new friends, Shenshen Wu, who was born in Taiwan and educated in Japan and in the United States, had a similar fate. In the Chinese culture, the oldest son is responsible for caring for the widowed mother. My friend was the only daughter, with three sibling brothers. When the oldest of the brothers called her to inform her that his wife was not willing to take on this care-giving chore, she asked him about the two other brothers. "No," he said, "none of these wives is willing. It seems to each of us that you would do the best job for our mother." Even though none of these wives had a busy career, they apparently felt that taking on this challenge would be too stressful for them. Shenshen was a chemist who had a successful career; she had invented a famous golf ball, called the Titleist. Her schedule was not only crowded but it required her to travel frequently. What should she do? In the past she had helped her husband care for his mother after this woman had became dependent. Now she could see no other solution to this issue, for although her calendar was full, she truly loved her mother, and therefore agreed to have her mother come to live with her so she could take care of her.

I met her mother. She was an elegant woman, very petite and very beautiful. Her courtly manners reflected the role she had lived as the gracious and elegant wife of a man who had served as Taiwan's ambassador to Japan. Shortly after she came to live with her daughter, she was diagnosed with Alzheimer's.

When I spoke privately with Shenshen's husband, Chang Ning, he sang his wife's praises, adding, "My wife was there to help me with my mother, I, in turn, will be there to help and support her." Husband and wife together, they cared for her mother with grace and dignity, until this elderly woman died. How I admired that couple!

As I began my research into the legal and medical details of Larry's illness, I learned, that at that time, neither Medicare nor our insurance company would pay for either his care or his medications, for at that time Alzheimer's was not considered to be a disease. Needless to say, accepting that information took a bit of adjusting on my part. Finally, I consulted a lawyer who specialized in marital assets. If I were willing to divorce Larry, some of our assets could be protected. The caveat, however, was that I would not be allowed to personally involve myself in my husband's care. This choice was unacceptable to me.

Because of these unhappy financial facts, I became, as one of my friends said, a member of the "impoverished gentry." Impoverished, however, is a relative term. In my case it means that expensive luxuries were not to be contemplated. Now, the value of our gifts to family members and friends would have to be geometrically reduced. Fortunately having enough funds to satisfy ordinary needs was not a serious concern. This was a time to remember what my father had always said; "One can arrive at the city near you, in one's small second-hand car, as soon as one's neighbor can arrive while he is driving his Bentley." This entailed an adjustment to the definition of our lifestyle but, because Larry's illness was to consume most of my time for the first thirteen years of his fifteen year illness, and even more so after he resided in an expensive care center, this change became almost automatic, because it was dictated by my husband's needs, and the time, energy, and financial resources needed to satisfy them.

Even after all the efforts I made to educate myself, I found myself at square one again, with only the Presence to help me. I understand that saying, "only the Presence," is not the correct theological thing to say, but it felt that way! I realized that the Presence had a lot more on his plate than just being concerned with my husband's illness and my care-giving issues. All over the world voices were crying out to him for succor, for help with their safety, their hunger and their homelessness. Child International and other groups are trying to solve these needs, but the numbers of those who suffer are countless, their needs multitudinous.

Would the Shepherd hear me now; would he help us now, and in all the years to come? I prayerfully hoped that he would do this for my husband and me.

My husband's illness never canceled out the validity of his humanity. Later in this book I discuss one example of the "voice" of humanity still alive in an apparently extremely damaged patient. This moment validated her personhood, and by instance, that of others with similar disorders, thus demonstrating that their conscious selves are still present within there disordered brains.

As any sailor knows, (and I was a sailor each summer in my childhood), it is critical to be aware of the tides and winds and the boats around you, and you must not forget to appoint a lookout if you have your spinnaker up! The Good Shepherd was to be my lookout, "As the coastlands wait for you're teaching," I thought, "so will I, as I set sail with your winds filling my sails."

The Good Shepherd would now be the most important member of my crew.

A Japanese proverb states, "When walked for love, a one thousand mile journey will seem as if it were only one mile".

Love can be that magical!

CHAPTER FIVE

Two Yellow Slickers

The summers in Vermont after Larry was diagnosed with Alzheimer's went smoothly. Taking advice from the book, "The 36-Hour Day", I had finally found someone to person-sit for Larry. She was familiar with the behavior of a patient with Alzheimer's. Her presence freed me to have occasional lunches with friends, to regularly attend my monthly spiritual book club, and once a week to trail-ride my mare, Gypsy. I called this exercise "Riding Zen". I would always return home from my weekly ride feeling mentally tranquil and physically energized. Larry and I continued to enjoy driving Gypsy together, entering several Carriage Driving Shows.

My garden to the right of our house was flourishing. This garden with its evergreens and flowers seemed to extend a welcome to passer-byes, as though saying, "Do stop and enter". We had extended the patio at the back of the house by moving the retaining wall that held back the bottom of Mt. Peg, which rose at a steep angle straight up behind our small yard. Although this entailed excavating ten feet into the hillside, it had the advantage of enlarging the patio and leaving us with a higher retaining wall that was the perfect height for sitting. With a few cushions added, we now had extra places for guests to sit down in comfort. This was important to me and to Larry, for entertaining friends in a casual manner was the best way to maintain normalcy.

The terrace at the back of the house was shady on hot days, but it was also confining. I had planted some Hosta, trailing Vinca, and European Ginger here and there on the hillside, making this area more attractive and inviting. An awning covered the area where we sat. It was very large and stretched straight out from the house to cover the entire flag-stoned patio area. Because the awning was operated with a motor it was easy for me to open and close it. We could sit out there on hot day and be sitting in the shade. If it was raining we were protected from the rain and therefore we could continue our Bar-B-Q gatherings. This patio was a pleasant spot, although not like the days when we lived in Bolton and had acres of land that Larry could explore at will.

I could not help remembering the days when my husband's space was not limited. He often went to Europe on company business. Over the years he became very friendly with Hildebrand Weber, who lived in Florence, Italy. Hildy was a true Renaissance man. He had a doctorate in economics and was a history buff. His home was filled with family paintings of the Masters especially of Canaletto's. Hildy was the travel companion 'par excellence' because of his knowledge of art and history. What an education we received as we took side-trips, spending time visiting places Hildy claimed were essential for us to experience.

My mind went back to a trip taken with Hildy to the Rimini area on the Adriatic Coast of Italy. Because my husband and

Hildy were busy consulting with a manufacturer I was free to visit places that I had read about. With a young woman acting as my interpreter we visited a tenth century Romanesque Church St. Appolonia was a small jewel. The wall behind the altar was covered with mosaics depicting Christ as the Good Shepherd holding a Lamb in his arms. Above the clear-storied windows on both sidewalls were at least fifteen life-sized sheep, progressing toward the Christ. These mosaics displayed a charming simplicity, depicting an almost child-like faith in this gentle caregiver.

On that day I was to meet the men for lunch at a seaside restaurant on the coast. This place was well known for its seafood. Our host, the factory owner Mr. Batastini, announced that we were about to enjoy thirty courses, including some of the most delicious and exotic fish from this part of Italy. My interpreter sat beside me, and I asked her not to tell me what I was eating until after I had consumed it. After six courses we then had what appeared to be rings fried in seasoned oil. After I had finished eating this course our host asked if I had enjoyed it. "Oh, yes, indeed, I did," I replied. He said he would ask the waiter to cook, for me, in any way I chose, another version of this famous seafood. I whispered to my guide, "What was it?" "Squid", she replied. Our host was conferring with the waiter and shortly after, an enormous platter was presented to me. On this platter rested a very large, very white, squid, whose eye was gazing up at me. Larry sometimes used squid as bait when fishing on the ocean. But, at that time, I had never seen squid on a menu, and certainly never had seen one this large. What to do? After a short pause I told our host, "I'm afraid if I eat that, I will not be able to enjoy the rest of this delicious meal." "Good answer" Maria, my interpreter whispered. Smiling happily, our host told the waiter to continue serving our thirty-course luncheon.

My host had, of course, succeeded in his "one-up-manship". Bringing in the largest squid of that day's catch, and watching my reaction, had added a special twinkle to his eyes.

Back at home in Vermont Larry fell down the stairs one night while trying to find his way to the second floor bathroom after making a left turn instead of a right turn. Luckily he was not seriously hurt when he fell, but it made me realize that a bit a remodeling was necessary. The next day I called a carpenter and a plumber asking them to transform one of the closets in the master bedroom into a half bath. When this work was finished I could lock the bedroom door at night, then Larry could easily find his way to this bath since it remained lit. Once he no longer had to search for the bath in the adjacent hall my sleepless nights were over.

We would often walk to town to look at the shops, to attend gallery openings, to visit our church in the late afternoon, and then, our last stop, to go to the ice cream store. These activities were keeping Larry's illness from progressing into the later stages of Alzheimer's. We were always together and had a full schedule. Not far from us was Hanover, New Hampshire where Dartmouth College is located. The college houses an excellent small museum. A short drive away from Hanover over the state line across the river into Vermont, there is a superb restaurant called, La Poole 'A Dents. Once a year this charming restaurant presented a reservation-only dinner in honor of the banquet in the short story "Babette's Feast". This meal exactly replicated the meal described in

Isaak Dinesen's story with the same wines accompanying each course. The evening was leisurely, beginning at 7:30 and lasting until the after dinner liqueurs had been consumed. Because we loved Isaak Dinesen's story we were especially pleased to attend this banquet.

Across from this restaurant was the Norwich Inn, which was decorated with original William Morris style wallpapers. We occasionally met friends there for lunch.

As part of our daily ritual we left our house at 5:00 each evening, accompanied by our toy poodle Babette, who walked down town with us to sit and meditate in our church. Trotting beside us Babette would accompany us following us into the pew, sitting up so straight and so attentively. She always faced the altar; never moving. But each day, and the timing was always the same, after about five minutes, she would stand up, shaking herself so energetically that her I.D. tags tinkled. Then she would turn and look back to the main doors, as though to say," There! That is all the time that I plan to spend today chatting with my Absolute Alpha." My husband and I would laugh at her, picked up her leash and walked out of the Church. After a stop for ice cream for all three of us we would wend our way home.

This schedule of occasional visits to art galleries, simple lunches in our town, having friends over for an uncomplicated supper, or attending the Fireman's annual Bar-B-Q, kept us active and healthy. This routine continued in the summers in Vermont for a total of twelve years. Larry seemed to be 'marching in place'. Because of Larry's tendency to wander I always accompanied him on any outings. We had a full schedule and these day-trips kept Larry mentally stimulated.

Yet, as the years past I noticed some of his abilities were diminishing. He no longer chose to read books and rarely liked to watch television. He did however still take pleasure in listening to music. His son Larry had given him a portable battery operated machine with attached earphones that played tapes of the jazz music that he loved. Now he could listen to his favorite music where and whenever he wished. Life in Vermont had to be more scheduled and more energetic than our winters in Florida because in Placida he could freely walk around the property and get his exercise that way. Because it was a gated community on the inter-coastal, there were always men in attendance at the entrance.

In two days we were scheduled to begin our drive south to our condo to spend the winter on the west coast of Florida. We had planned stops at Williamsburg and Georgia on our way south before we would eventually arrive at our Placida Harbor home.

Before leaving I had prepared the house for our extended absence. The water was turned off, and all the other household chores were completed. Even the car would be packed the evening before our departure! Everything would be ready for our morning drive.

Leaving at 9:00 a.m. we stopped off twice to rest, to eat, and to walk around a bit. I was particularly happy that we had planned to visit Williamsburg. So much of our national history had begun there. When we arrived the manager of our hotel told us that a video was available in our room that told the history of the town and the lives of all the important people connected with the Revolution. After settling in we watched this video. Larry and I were particularly impressed to learn how much wealth these men had, and how much they stood to lose personally if the Revolution had failed. They deserve their hero status in our history, for the risks they took were enormous.

The next morning, after breakfast, we went to spend the day at Williamsburg. I was excited because I love the architecture of that period, and the gardens would be well worth a thoughtful stroll. We stopped first at their gift shop where I bought a generous sized book about Williamsburg.

The Town Hall there was large and elegant, and the houses had an understated quiet dignity to them. I wanted to visit the interior of one of these homes because the guidebook said that this house had a large collection of Chinese porcelain, something my grandmother had collected. But Larry said he was not interested in joining me. "I will wait for you on this bench," he said. "All right dear," I replied, "I will only be inside for a short time. So wait here for me."

When I came out of the building Larry was nowhere to be found. At first I thought I should stay there in case Larry showed up. But as the minutes flew by I realized I needed help. As I looked around I saw a man with a Williamsburg I.D. on his lapel, and his name written under it. I approached him and said, "Jim, my husband is missing. He was to wait here for me, but it seems that he has wandered off. Unfortunately he has Alzheimer's, so I am worried that he may wander too far." "What is he wearing?" Jim asked, "He has khaki pants on and a blue Lacoste shirt." I replied. As we both looked around at the visitors we noticed many men dressed just like that. "Does he have anything different about his appearance?" Jim asked. "Yes, he has a mustache, he wears eye-glasses, and his name is Larry," I replied. Jim then took his radiophone and called his headquarters to send out an alarm for a missing person giving them the description I had given him. Two hours later Jim's radiophone rang. "We have a gentleman here who tells us his wife Philomene is missing". "What is his name" Jim asked. "His name is Larry" was the reply. Jim told the caller where he was and to bring Larry to him. "I have been looking everywhere for you Phil" Larry said when he arrived. I had to think long and hard about the implications of this turn of events. I had forgotten how supervised our expeditions had been in Vermont. Needless to say, I decided that I would never allow Larry out of my sight from then on.

It was a sunny that day in Williamsburg, and we had found Larry well and unharmed. I had much to be grateful for. On the minus side, what I now know about this historic place I learned from the book that I purchased that day in the gift shop at Williamsburg.

From Williamsburg we planned to drive to Georgia, stopping at a motel there, before continuing on to the Gulf Coast. That would enable us to arrive at our Condo the following day. I decided not to let Larry drive again because he had made some potentially serious mistakes in the past week. My Williamsburg experience had been a "Heads Up" moment.

The next morning we set off, finally arriving in Georgia at a nice motel. Having stopped off for supper we could settle in right away. As I started to search for our pajamas I realized that I was running low on cigarettes. "Larry dear," I said, "would you please go to the motel office and ask them where the nearest store is that sells cigarettes?" "O.K." he replied, "happy to do that." At last I could stretch out my legs and relax on a comfortable chair.

After a short time I sat straight up and exclaimed, "Larry", where was he? I looked at my watch. He had left at five and now it was six. I decided to check out the lobby. Perhaps he was having coffee there. But no, when I got there he was nowhere in sight. I became very concerned. As I stood outside the motel office I noticed, for the first time, that our car was missing. Then I remembered the incident at Williamsburg and realized that I needed help. Why had I not thought to take away Larry's car keys? I went back into the office and told the manager that I needed help. After I explained to him what had happened, he suggested that I call the State Police. I called and was told that a State Trooper would come to talk with me.

When he arrived I tried to control my surprise, for he was so good looking that he could have been a famous actor. He was better looking than Denzel Washington! This Trooper was charming and intelligent and asked me significant questions. He then picked up the office phone and called in an all-state bulletin on Larry and our automobile. He told me his name was Robert and he would be staying with me until Larry was located. I welcomed this news for I was really petrified, not knowing what might happen to my husband. "Let's go back to your room and wait. Headquarters will call there if they have any news." Robert said. He was excellent at making conversation. He asked about my family and told me about his family. He asked what my husband had done in his business life and spoke of the day-to-day happenings in his life as a state trooper. It was now 1:00 a.m. in the morning and there was still no news. I felt sorry for Robert. Even on a train ride one could talk to a seatmate for just so long. Every once in a while Robert would check with his command unit.

At 2:30 a.m. Robert asked for the alarm to be extended to South Carolina.

At 5:30 Robert asked for the alarm to be extended to North Carolina.

At 8:00 a.m. the phone rang. "Where did you say you were calling from?" Robert asked. And then he listened for several minutes. When he hung up he told me what had been said. It seems that Larry had checked in to a four star hotel in North Carolina. Then, at 6: 30, he had gone down to the lobby to get coffee and pastry. While he was there a State trooper had entered to get his morning coffee. The trooper overheard Larry saying that his wife was missing. "Where are you from?" asked the trooper. "Massachusetts" Larry replied. "What town?" Larry answered, "Bolton?" "What street?" asked the Trooper. "I do not know. But our next-door neighbor just lost her husband due to a brain tumor, and she has a small child named Amanda." So the trooper in North Carolina placed a call to the Chief of Police in Bolton and asked whether he could recognize the people Larry had just described. "Yes," said the police chief, "I can". He gave the trooper the telephone number of Amanda's house. When the trooper connected with Amanda's mother, Janet, she told him that I always called her each day to tell her where we were staying, and yes she had the number for the motel in Georgia.

"This is such good news," I said. "Let's go out for coffee and celebrate." Robert agreed. We went to the office and had fruit, coffee, rolls and jelly. While we were eating Robert told me that he had stayed with me because his captain was afraid that my husband would drive off the road in the dark and might even end up eaten by an alligator. "I am so glad that you did not tell me that last night," I said, with a sigh. Then Robert and I laughed, releasing the tension of our all night vigil. After several cups of coffee Robert and I went back to the room to wait for Larry.

As I entered the room I noticed that my handbag had been opened, and all the contents were spewed over the top of the bed. I then checked my wallet. No money and no credit cards either. It was so bizarre I could not stop laughing. "No one will ever believe me. While having coffee with a State Trooper I was robbed of all my money and all my credit cards." Robert too was laughing. "I will talk to the credit card people for you. And the state has money for travelers in trouble, so I can get you gas and lunch money."

At 10:00 a.m. my husband arrived with a State Police car escorting him. At each new state line the Troopers from the next state had taken over starting when they left North Carolina, and switching again as they reached Georgia. At last, they arrived at the motel; Larry had "found" his wife.

I was relieved and happy to see my husband, and embarrassed that I had not taken seriously the Williamsburg "heads up" experience. I was also saddened to realize that the progression of his Alzheimer's had take a more serious turn.

The next day we stopped at a shop that sold marine supplies. They had yellow slickers that were waterproof and sturdy enough to wear on boats. I bought one for each of us. These slickers served for many years as a way for Larry to find me and for me to keep tabs on him.

At last we arrived at our condo on the Gulf Coast and our winter vacation began.

I did not forget to remove the car keys from Larry's key chain.

CHAPTER SIX

Someone To Talk To

Our Georgia adventure made me feel as though I had survived a session with Outward Bound. I could relax now that we were home in our Florida condo, on familiar turf. Larry continued his morning visits to all the hibiscus plants in our condo association, choosing the perfect flowers to bring back to me. He would present them to me in such a courtly manner. In 1993 Larry was in the tenth year of his illness. So far the only concern I had was his tendency to wander away from home base. But here in Placida we were located where most of the residents knew him, and would watch out for him. The men who guarded the entry gate and the captain on the ferry were aware of his tendency to wander, so I had auxiliary eyes. For the first time in many days, I could relax.

It was a mild and sun-drenched afternoon the Tuesday when we went to enjoy a walk on the barrier-island beach. We watched the small shore birds that were running to and fro, managing to escape the waves of the incoming tide. On this day, as we made our way north along the beach, we would pause intermittently to select a small scallop shell for our collection. Several hours later, holding each other's hands, we ambled back to the dock to wait for the ferry to take us to the mainland. When it arrived we boarded and prepared to enjoy the short trip back to our condo on the mainland. As the boat made its way east we kept a practiced eye out for any Osprey that might be hunting for food. We spotted one, circling high up above us looking down at the water. Suddenly it dove straight down from a great height and caught a sizable fish for its young chicks. We were thrilled to witnesses this event. After the boat landed we leisurely walked back to our condo. People said we were a handsome couple. Larry was tall with the lean body of an athlete, while I was small with green eyes and a steely grey head of hair. As we strolled along the walkway toward our condo we talked together about our plans to celebrate our fortieth wedding anniversary in March with all our children and grandchildren. Each family would have their own condo. They would all stay on the beach providing the older and younger generation with an oceanfront vacation and time to re-connect with one-another, for these families were spread geographically far and wide.

Once Larry and I returned to our condo we each took a quick shower to wash off the sand and the salt from our visit to the beach. Now we could relax together, sitting on the lounge chairs on our lanai facing the inter-coastal waters. Late afternoon was the best time to enjoy the parade of sailboats and cruisers as they passed through the drawbridge that was a one-half mile south of our porch. It was fun to watch the boat's as they slowly made there way north toward their homeports.

Later we toasted the sunset that this day flooded the sky and the waters with reds and oranges and yellows, slowly fading to soft mauve streaked with a deep gold and magenta.

Gradually, as the sky darkened, the stars would appear, clear and twinkling. But on this night there was no moon.

At times I would invite a few of our friends to join us for cocktails. These friends were aware of Larry's illness, which took the tension out of the late afternoon, and made for a pleasant get-together. Today however, we were sitting by ourselves, enjoying some snacks with our soft drinks.

"I miss my dog Bantry" Larry said to me, "I wish we could get a new Border Collie to replace him." "You know that our condo association regulates the size of the dog allowed here." I responded, "One may not have a dog that weighs more than twenty-five pounds." After a long pause Larry said, "I still wish we could find a dog like Bantry. He was always right beside me whenever I was fly-fishing on the pond. Do you remember how he never failed to bark his approval each time that I hooked a brown trout? Whenever we rode our horses together on the trails and through the woods Bantry was always with us, running circles around us. And too, in the evenings, when I sat on the couch, he would push aside the person sitting next to me with his wet nose and make a place for himself, so he could curl up next to me. Bantry was such a loyal companion." Larry now sat quietly for a time, sipping his Pepsi, looking out across the water, seemingly content. "Phil, how much do you think Jacques weighs?" He suddenly asked. Jacques was a Toy Poodle belonging to a friend. He was a handsome black dog, but not well behaved. "I didn't realize that you liked Jacques," I mused. "Well he is a smart dog, and he is quite small. He must not weigh too much!" my husband pointed out. "That's true." I murmured. "Could we find a dog like Jacques for me?" Larry asked.

This was a difficult request for me to agree to. In my mind I had always considered Toy Poodles to be some kind of wind-up toy. Jacques, for example, was constantly barking and occasionally nipping at people's heels. He had been thoroughly spoiled, and not surprisingly, he was not the sort of dog one would be pleased to have as one's own. For me, a poodle, no matter what size, was a fool of a dog, and I wanted none of it.

All our Border Collies like Bantry, had been well behaved. Once these dogs realized that the rules were determined by their alphas, they quickly learned to comply, knowing that there was no negotiating or exception to these rules. They understood that chasing cars, bicycles or horses was not allowed; herding wild turkeys, and herding children who were swimming in our pond was also against the rules. Barking to announce the presence of strangers or visitors on the property was allowed; but only long enough to get the attention of their owners. We had owned several dogs of this breed over those past years, because, although I will admit they did occasionally choose to disobey the rules, they were always intelligent, loyal and fun to be with. On the other hand, I felt, that a Toy Poodle's diminutive size would only maximize the embarrassment that owning such a dog would impose.

Still, I did not have it in my heart to refuse Larry his request. In recent months his life had changed dramatically. He could no longer enjoy so many of his past pleasures. His Alzheimer's had now progressed into the early middle stages, playing tennis and even fly-fishing was, sadly and regrettably, beyond his capabilities and Larry was, unfortunately, keenly aware of the erosion of his mental capacities. Although he was able to converse with our friends and did enjoy participating in social events he still could not accept these changes which were happening to him, and this seriously concerned him. My husband asked for so little of me. Having his own companion dog was one of the few things he truly wanted. So, at last, but halfheartedly, I agreed to search for a breeder of Toy Poodles who had healthy and well-socialized puppies.

Eventually we did find such a breeder, just one hour north of where we lived. The puppy's parents were also there, on the premises, so I could evaluate their temperaments. When I called for an appointment the owner mentioned that we would have to be interviewed first, before we could see any of her dogs. "My dogs are special," the owner of the kennel said, "They are intelligent and are given a great deal of individual attention. Their parents are both champions and have always produced healthy dogs. I am particular about the type of homes my puppies go to. So you can understand why I want to meet with you."

This conversation concerned me. Would the breeder object to placing a puppy in our home because of Larry's Alzheimer's? This was obviously not something that I could discuss with my husband. So I decided to keep the appointment, and hope that if the breeder felt that our home was not suitable she would tactfully tell us that all of her puppies were now spoken for.

When we arrived at the kennel Larry was at his best. He asked the breeder many questions about the breed, such as how did she choose the dogs that she intended to breed, and whether the color of the puppies was always the same as that of the parents. I called this behavior "Larry on automatic pilot". This skill had been practiced each day of his career when he frequently mixed with people who were attending business or social events. Larry had always been fascinated with people; he loved learning about their lives, their families and their work, and he always remembered their names and their interests. It was a blessing that Larry still retained these social skills for it made my life so much less complicated.

Even now, at cocktail parties at our Club House in Florida, Larry's conversational skills impressed newcomers. After one party my good friend, Linda Smith, mentioned to a new resident, that it was unfortunate that Larry had Alzheimer's. That gentleman remarked that he found nothing wrong with Larry, and that perhaps it was his wife who needed help. When I heard this, I thought, "In Vino Veritas" (there is truth in wine). Reflecting on my own faults and shortcomings, and my inadequacies for the challenges that faced me in the future, I felt that this man had a point. But my husband's ability to cover-up his mental losses was truly amazing.

Thankfully, at the kennel, our interview with the breeder went well. She then left us to bring the parents of the puppies into the room. They trotted in with their tails wagging, letting us pat them and talk to them. These dogs did not seem overly anxious for attention. Although they did not bark at us they were very curious about us, and inspected us carefully, almost as though they too were checking out our credentials! I was surprised to find the word 'dignified' coming to mind, although I wondered if one could assign this adjective to a dog.

The breeder then asked us what sex we were considering. I responded, "A female." "I have only one female," the breeder said, "I will bring her in after I return the parents to their play area."   Soon a small bit of black fluff came scrambling into the room and made straight for Larry. "That is a good sign," I supposed. When Larry picked up the puppy she licked his face, and then snuggled sweetly against his neck. No question that this little dog liked what she tasted and smelled. My husband was happy to hear that this puppy was now to be his dog.

On the way home we discussed a name for the puppy. "She is a French dog," I commented "and probably should have a French name". As we drove south we thought of French names from history and also from stories that we had read in the past. "I remember reading that one of the Queens of France had a puppy named Nicole" I remarked. "I remember when years ago we read the story "Babette's Feast", Larry said, "and I think that Babette will be a good name." So that name was chosen for the new puppy.

Four weeks later we brought the new puppy home. She was immediately solicitous of her new master. She would sit on his lap and listen to him talk and then voice her approval with soft noises. "I do so love this dog" Larry would cheerfully call to me." She is as intelligent as was my dog Bantry" he would declare. I now realized that buying a Toy Poodle had been the right decision after all. During the next several years I would call this sweet dog to my side and tell her, "Go do your job." She would then trot eagerly to her master and sit with him attentively, keeping him company. If Larry asked her to dance for him she would dance with enthusiasm, much like a circus dog. If he asked her to say "please" for her treat she would beg so dramatically that it brought laughter to all who beheld her. If he asked her to snuggle she would jump to the top of the couch, sit with her head close to his, cross her paws and assume a regal pose. Babette was ever considerate of Larry's every wish, always responding with devotion and apparent joy. She was the perfect companion dog for her new master.

CHAPTER SEVEN

Beauty In Brokenness

"Don't forget Babette's leash," Larry called. "Thanks for the reminder," I replied, "Everything we need is in the wicker basket by the front door." Because our folding chairs were stored at the Island's Clubhouse all we would ordinarily need to carry on the ferry were the beach towels and our sunblock. But today, because our oldest son and his wife were visiting with their daughter Katherine we made sure to bring the beach toys, which we had purchased especially for this grandchild.

Larry and I visited this beach as often as the weather and our schedules permitted. Today we were especially pleased to share the beach with our handsome son, Larry Jr. who was a tall man with a matchless sense of humor. When he was small he was a toe-head, his hair had now darkened to a soft brown. His lovely wife Michelle was a petite woman with naturally blonde hair and blue eyes. I secretly called her," God's gift to a mother-in-law." She had such a serene personality and was always generous with her time and talent. We were to meet them at the dock because they were staying in a different condo in the same association for one week.

Our Granddaughter Kate was delighted to learn that she would be riding on a ferryboat to reach our island. The ferry was moored at the landing in the association's small harbor on the mainland. It was a pontoon type boat accommodating about twenty passengers. The fifteen-minute ride across the inter-coastal waters would be an adventure for this child.

As soon as all the passengers were on board the captain untied the mooring lines and started the engine. As the boat made its way across the water the Captain called out to Kate, "Look over this side of the boat and watch for the Porpoises as they come along side." When she spotted them she clapped her hands and exclaimed, "Oh, they are so big, and look how shiny they are." Her father held her as she bent down trying to touch these elegant creatures. "This trip is so much more entertaining with a child on board," one of the passengers commented. All the others nodded and smiled in agreement.

As the ferry approached the dock on the Island Kate's anticipation grew. The barrier island beach was seven miles long, its white sands covered with numerous shells at low tide. It was the perfect place to discover colorful shells and shark's teeth. Scuffing our feet as we all moved forward, and leaning over we concentrated on our search. Larry Jr. and Michelle led the way and I followed them. My husband and Katherine ambled behind.

We had been collecting shells for quite some time. I brought our finds back to our condo and placed the scallops within the glass lamp in our bedroom, capturing their beauty and variety. I placed the shark's teeth in a crystal bowl on our coffee table. We had been extremely selective, choosing only perfect scallops with unbroken shoulders. I prized the magenta shells as well as the rare yellow ones because these colors complemented the décor in our bedroom.

This hunt also provided us with our daily constitution. Now and then we would pause in our search to chat with our acquaintances. Larry could discuss fly-fishing with the men, and I would introduce our visitors to the women, and share a laugh with them over our mutual "shell seeking" addiction.

Soon, however, our bedroom lamp would be filled, but we knew that we had other reasons to continue this hunt. Residents who had been coming here for many seasons saved their extra shells and shark's teeth. They bagged these finds and kept them hidden, ready to be used later when they would secretly salt the beach for their guests; thus making it possible for their family and friends to enjoy the thrill of discovering for themselves these delicate gifts from the sea.

Larry preferred the seashore in the wintertime. When our children were young we often took them skiing, but winter sports were not the activities that Larry would have chosen for himself. He would rather play indoor tennis with his sons; and did so when the boys were older. Before Larry's father died at age forty-two, his family had lived, for a number of years, in the Caribbean, because his father, Lawrence, was a Dental Surgeon, a Lt. Commander in the U.S. Navy, he was stationed at a naval base there. Those years for Larry were some of the most meaningful of his childhood, for he was only twelve years old when his father, Lawrence, died. Therefore, Larry associated the Florida climate with his childhood memories of his father.

At the time of Kate's visit Larry was in the very early middle stages of Alzheimer's. It was a blessing that we were able to continue our walks on our beach. One of the common vexations of Alzheimer's patients is their tendency to wander, sometimes for great distances. Oddly, they often walk in a straight line in one direction. Because our beach was on an Island, Larry could not get too far away if he decided to explore on his own, and he could be located within a short time. Relieved of this worry I could relax in the perfections of these surroundings.

But then, one day, a week before our son and his family came to visit the guard at the gate called me. "Are you aware that Larry has taken the ferry to the beach?" he asked, "The boat captain radioed me and asked me to call you and tell you." I immediately called my friends trying to recruit bodies for a search team. All these kind people met at the ferry dock to wait for the return trip. As the ferry pulled into the dock the Captain was motioning with "two thumbs up." After the ferry was secured, he walked over to me and said, "Larry says he was looking for you." And there he was, walking off the ferry. We all applauded with joy and with relief.

Although my husband's interest in picking perfect shells had waned, in his own way he still enjoyed the process. His choice of shells however, had radically changed; now he would select ones that were broken and eaten away by the erosive action of the waves and the abrasive rubbings of the sands. Even though this troubled me I continued to help him, putting his chosen shells into his net bag, and then holding the bag in the ocean to allow the waves to wash away the sands hiding within these shells. I had managed to control my feelings of humiliation and concern over this issue, and quietly attempted to convince my husband that these shells were blemished and therefore not appropriate for our collection. But Larry remained determined to collect these broken shells. "I want to keep this particular type of shell," he explained, "I like them because each one is unique."

By now I had learned to save my energy for the battles that really mattered, such as driving our car and other important issues. My friend had recently given me a piece of advice. "If you are not willing to die on the battlefield over a certain issue," Peggy Lannon said, "then have the wisdom to withdraw, and let that issue remain unchallenged." Shell collecting was one of the times when I considered this advice useful and put it to practice.

Once we were back in our condo, however, and as soon as I was by myself, I would throw his shells into the trash. In my opinion these shells were definitely not keepers. I had a healthy dose of German genes, and perfection was something that I naively believed was achievable.

Was it also possible that these shells were becoming, for me, a symbol of the deterioration that my husband's illness was causing in his brain? Tossing these shells away may have been a subconscious effort, on my part, to hide from the realities of Larry's situation. I never confided to any of my friends how I felt about Larry's choice of damaged shells. I was too embarrassed by these feelings, and ashamed to become aware of the anger that I occasionally felt toward Larry, because his illness was causing so many unfortunate changes in our lifestyle.

Later that year, after we had returned to our home in the north for the summer, and I had spent a day at a workshop for caregivers of persons with advanced middle-stage Alzheimer's,

I learned enough to begin to comprehend why I had all these feelings.

One of the attendees at this workshop was a gentleman who was the caregiver for his wife. He was tall and handsome, well dressed and well spoken, with silver hair that gave him an elegant look. This man was witty and incredibly inventive in his approach to his daily dilemmas "Two skills are absolutely essential to survive as sole caregiver with your sanity intact," John said, "One must learn to see humor in almost every situation, and one must approach difficult moments with a "what if" slant to ones thinking. For example, one could achieve the best results by doing something in an unexpected way. I call it utilizing an inside-out way of thinking." Then he continued with this reminder, "Never forget the cathartic release of laughter."

This man charmed us all. He then told us how he solved the problem he was having when it came time to give his wife a shower. She was determined not to remove her clothes before stepping into the shower. He had tried, many times and in numerous ways to persuade her to disrobe, but she adamantly refused. So he decided on the principle of "if you can't beat 'em, then join 'em" to let her go into the shower stall with her clothes on. Once she was inside he would turn on the hand-held shower and thoroughly wet her down. Naturally she objected to standing in wet clothes, so he cheerfully helped her to remove them. Then he took an extra large spray bottle, which he had found in a tack shop, and filled it with a type of baby-no-tears shampoo, and sprayed her hair and all over her body. After this application he rinsed her clean, towel dried her and promptly re-dressed her in clean clothes. He had

had the foresight to purchase three sets of leisure clothes, all in the same color, so when he re-dressed her the dry clothes exactly matched the wet ones that he had removed before he showered her. Needless to say, he was especially pleased to hear his wife say, "Thank you dear, these are my favorite clothes."

I found this man's advice to be priceless. "Never disagree," I remembered him saying, "Just find a new way to think about it, and address it as a new set of issues to be resolved."

I remembered the years when I was tending to a series of toddlers and how this gentleman's approach had worked wonders for me with those determined souls. From that time on I had many occasions to celebrate this amusing way of dealing with vicissitudes.

I did not, however, have this insight at the time of my granddaughter Kate's visit. At that time it was my five-year old grandchild who taught me another new way of seeing.

I often referred to Katherine as my gingersnap grandchild; she was an attractive child with reddish-blonde hair, blue eyes and a sprinkle of cinnamon colored freckles across her nose and cheeks. This emotional child was intelligent, charming and especially quick to sense the feelings of others. Also, at times, and alas, she was quick to express her disagreements with the world around her.

But on this sunny day Kate was gaily skipping across the sand beside her grandfather, as they looked for shells together. I watched as Larry reached down to choose a shell and then showed it to his granddaughter. "Oh Granddaddy," she cried with an ecstatic look on her face, "You picked one that shows the inside of the shell! Isn't it beautiful? Can you find one just like that for me?" Then I saw Larry smile at Kate with such joy in his eyes. Turning toward her he bent over and kissed her. Then he held out his hand and offered her the shell that he had just found. "This one is for you," he said. "Oh thank you granddaddy," Kate answered, "I will keep it forever as my very own."

The next morning my son took his family to Sarasota so Kate could enjoy the Mote museum of sharks and aquatic fish. Larry and I decided to take the earliest ferry to the beach. A storm the night before meant the shell seeking would be exceptional.

The light on the beach after a storm was so beautiful; it seemed to surround everything around us with a softness seldom seen. As we started our walk we saw a large conch shell lying there. It stood out against the wet sand where the motion of the ebbing tide had placed it. The early morning light cast a golden glow around it so that it seemed to float, suspended above the froth left behind by the waves. I stood there for a moment listening to the sea sounds that seemed to sigh a requiem for this shell. I wanted to reach down and touch that shell, to examine it, and to let it sing its sad and solemn dirge. But I could not. To possess it meant that I must concede the validity of its fragmentation. All over the surface of this shell was the history of its loss. No longer would the sound of the sea sing within it because there was too much destruction. Its surface was eroded and in some places it was completely broken and shattered by the very ocean that had been its home. It was isolated from all that gave it energy. The creature that had lived within it was no longer there. And the sea, that abundant breast that had been its life's source, had forcibly rejected it. I crouched beside this shell. I was shaken by the tale it told and still unable to touch it. Touching would be an acknowledgement of the rightness of the seas rhythm, of this cyclic motion that is eternal and inevitable. I felt as though the angry waves from the storm that had passed had found a home in my heart. "This should not be," I thought, "This must not be. There is no purpose to this disintegration. To have the history of so much suffering displayed in such a way is an obscenity." I could not hold my head up. I was bowed down, refusing to assent to this reality.

At that moment Larry reached down and lifted up this shell. He held it out to me. The early morning light shone salmon on his face and on the shell he offered me. I looked up at him and saw such an overwhelming beauty there. "For you dear, to photograph," he said. I stretched out my hands to receive his gift. I thought, "I must hold this shell, embrace it, and see it as he sees it. I will respond with love to this now rare expression of his love for me. Touching the pitted surface of this shell I will remember the years when he was there for me; my companion, my friend, my lover, a part of my very soul.

Only those who knew him in the past could understand what a wondrous treasure now rested so still, so fragile in my hands. He had given me his heart to hold.

That was the day when I began to happily help Larry collect his special shells with a new appreciation for the beauty to be found there within them. This moment re-emphasized that unique gift to me from my darling granddaughter Katherine. This experience, then, was a distinctly unique explication. This moment was the apex of my sea change.

For months after this day I would take these shells and dye them in red to bring out some of the warm tones in them. Sometimes I would highlight their shapes with gold and other colors to create a miniature sculpture. I strung some of them with thin gold yarn that I braided and formed into "chains" to hang them. Some I put in windows, and I strung one for Linda Smith to wear as jewelry. Was I trying to create an art form that would change the perspective of Larry's illness? Was I searching for something that would give meaning to the process of Larry's journey, something that would make it more acceptable?

Whatever my purpose for these shells, I now understood that each was a unique marvel. They were, as Larry had said, very definitely worth collecting. The beauty they expressed within them was absolutely varied.

One of the brightest of my remembrances over that long care-giving time was of that day, on that beach when we were collecting shells with our granddaughter.

In my memory I often recount what happened then, as I had watched Larry, walking with his granddaughter, and saw him leaning down to choose one particular shell and I remember how, after first giving a kiss to her, he gave her that shell to keep as her very own. Sweet Kate had gifted her grandfather with her exuberant approval of, and delight in his choice of that special shell. She had thus enabled Larry to graciously acknowledge her loving approval, and bestow in return, as his gift to her, a particular shell that contained so much beauty within its brokenness: a beauty that was recognized and appreciated by both of them.

CHAPTER EIGHT

Darkness At Noon

It was early May in 1997 and we were back again in Vermont, having returned, once again, from Florida. I had been successfully caring for Larry in our home for thirteen years.

However, each day something new in my husband's behavior surprised and concerned me. One evening, as I was preparing dinner, Larry called to me, "Phil, please come here, I need to talk to you." So I went into the living room and sat next to him. "Those three people sitting across from us," he whispered, "I do not want to eat with them. Could you ask them to go?" I looked across the room, but there was no one there. Then I remembered the successful method I had used to banish an imaginary lion which my nephew Ned "saw" in his bedroom while visiting us when he was quite small. I decided to give that technique a try in this situation. I got up, went across the room, shook hands with each "man", and said, "It was so nice of you to come to call on us. We are about to have our dinner, so I shall say goodbye to you, and walk you to the door." I walked to the door, opened it, waved goodbye, and then closed the door." "Thank you dear" Larry said. This was the first of a series of hallucinations that my husband experienced.

Another day, Larry asked me if he could take Babette with him downtown for a walk alone, without me accompanying him. I told him no, not at that time.

He suddenly became enraged, saying, "I will go out on my own if I want to". Then he had picked up an antique iron shoe-last that we used as a doorstop which must have weighed at least ten pounds. Larry raised it up high and then threw it down with force, carefully aiming at my head. I could feel the wind as it passed by my cheek, missing my head by inches. Larry had finally realized that the front door was locked and could only be opened with a key. He had free access to the back yard but the fence was five feet high and the gate had a combination lock on it. He now understood that he was locked in, and therefore deprived of his freedom to walk alone anywhere he chose to go.

The next week we had another disagreement. He became enraged and he pushed me down the front stairs. I painfully landed on my hip on the flag-stoned front hall floor. Oh my, it hurt! My first thought was, "What would happen to Larry if I had broken my hip?" This was my second serious "heads up." I could no longer safely take care of Larry at home alone. I would have to make other plans for his care.

To move my husband to a care facility I knew, that in the State of Vermont I would have to take out a Guardianship. When one applies for this position of guardian a Judge must send two Guardian Ad Litem lawyers to one's residence to act as protector of the rights of the individual who is to be "guarded".

Because I was not sure how my husband would react to the news that a guardianship was being taken out, and I was quite concerned that he might react with anger and violence, I had asked my son Larry Jr. and our friend Dean Goodwin to come to be there before the lawyers arrived in order to have helpful "muscles" available should we need to placate or restrain my husband.

The lawyers arrived and spoke with Larry first asking him about his war experience. These men were in their late twenties and war, for them, was something one watched on PBS or the history channel. When answering them Larry told them that he served first in a submarine, then in the navy air corps, and then, finally, he told them that he had served in the navel supply corps. Only this last part was true. His submarine story was an exact telling of the experience of one of his best friends. His navy air corps story was an exact telling of our friend John Meharg's war experience. John had been awarded the Navy Cross for his service during the war. When Larry had served in the supply corps he was stationed on a battleship, which was the true part of his story, but much less glamorous than were the two previous jobs that he had described. It had amazed me that these two men obviously believed my husband.

At that point the lawyers began to carefully, and slowly explain to Larry what a Guardianship was, and what it could necessitate. Larry listened with great interest. Suddenly Larry jumped up, screaming, "No Way! This is my house. I will make my own decisions. I will kill you Phil to prevent this from happening." He then darted across the room, grabbed me by the throat, lifting me up and out of my chair, and started to choke me. Young Larry and Dean tried unsuccessfully to make him release me.

"Dad, Ice Cream" our son finally said, "Let's go get ice cream, Dad." When young Larry said that, ("ice cream"), his father let go of me and slowly walked to the front door. My son and Dean followed him and took him down town to get his favorite treat.

There is no way to describe the tumult of emotions that I felt at that moment.

I looked over at the lawyers and saw them cell-phoning the Judge, saying, "We have an emergency here, your honor. We need an immediate Guardianship."

After the lawyers had left, and Dean and both Larrys had returned, I walked downtown to the Courthouse to meet with the Judge. He helped me to complete the forms that were required to arrange a guardianship over Larry. The Judge also arranged for Larry to be admitted to the Brattleboro Retreat. He arranged for Larry to be transported in an ambulance because he did not feel that I could safely drive him by myself.

Now a new stage of Larry's journey was to begin. We were to be separated for the remainder of his life. Soon we would learn what this new development would entail for both of us. But at this moment I knew that this day was surely our darkest day.

It seemed to me that neither the sun, nor the moon, nor the stars would be visible for us, for the heavens above must be heavy with the blackest of clouds filling the firmament as they raced across the skies above us.

Did my husband feel abandoned by me and by God? Did he question the justice of his affliction? Did he ask God, "Why?

For what reason is this tribulation being thrust upon me?" I do not know, for Larry never discussed this with me. What amazing grace was given to him so that he could continue to rely on the Good Shepherd to support him in these dark moments? Was he resigned to his fate? I think his behavior over the months when he resided there illustrated that he never approved of his fate and may have caused him to call out in anguish to God, yet he was eventually able to accept his fate because he was not alone on this journey for the Presence walked with him and consoled him.

All through that long day, after seeing Larry situated in the brain disorder unit at the Hospital in Brattleboro, I felt, as Larry must have felt, that God had abandoned us. It was impossible, on that day, for me to remember that we were not alone, for even the Presence seemed to have left us, taking His Light with Him.

CHAPTER NINE

Wonderous Moments

Our toy poodle, Barbette continued her caring behavior toward her master whenever she visited Larry at the Brattleboro Retreat. This delightful dog behaved like a well-trained therapy dog; her instincts were so correct. As soon as I stepped off the elevator on Larry's floor accompanied by Babette, this energetic little dog went about dancing and smiling and performing her tricks to entertain everyone there. She seemed to know that these patients needed her attention. The patients sat in their chairs along both sides of that long corridor waiting patiently for Babette to visit them. She allowed each of them to chat with her and gently pat her.

But her special attention was reserved for her master. She would sit on his lap and snuggle and kiss him and speak to him, bringing great joy to Larry. The entire time that Babette was there not one of the patients would complain or call out for help of any kind because all eyes were on this exuberant, and friendly dog. The nurses and aids loved her visits. When I arrived with Babette one of the aids would say, "Tea time," and smile in our direction. Once Babette was there they could relax and enjoy the fresh pastry treats I brought for them.

It may be possible that Babette became such a special dog because I kept instructing her that she was not a Poodle, but was really a Border Collie. Whatever the reason, she was the most exceptional Toy Poodle that I have ever known.

Almost every time we visited we would have to watch out for an elderly woman who was seated in a wheeled chair-walker. This patient would rush at top speed back and forth along the very long corridor, using her feet as her motor. She would not change directions for any obstacle or person in her path, not even for the nurse who was pushing the medication cart. For some reason she presumed that carts or people would move out of her way. Yet, each time she was near to Larry, when he had Babette sitting on his lap, she would pause in her marathon and gaze at them, with the sweetest expression on her face.

One day she stopped at the end of that long corridor, which was her usual place to pause and rest, and called out, "Doggy! Doggy! Come here doggy, I pat you." I felt pity and compassion for this strange woman, so I leashed Babette and started to walk down the long hall toward the woman in the walker. "Be careful Phil," Clare said, "she can be violent.' I replied, "Babette always seems to know how close she can go to people." So I led Babette down the corridor to meet this lady. Babette did come close to this woman, rubbing against her legs and finally she rested her head on this woman's knees. The woman leaned down from her seat in the walker and gently touched the dog. "Oh thank you doggy! Nice doggy. Is it all right for me to pat you?" Babette then lifted her head up and put her front paws up onto the woman's knees so this woman could pat her head and her neck. As I watched the two together I saw a beatific smile on the woman's face. I felt so sad for her for she seemed to be so alone, and no one was there to hug her and listen to her. As Babette and I left this woman and started to walk back toward Larry the woman called out, "Thank you doggy dear."

Then the head nurse, with tears in her eyes, came up to me and said, "That woman has been here with us for three years and has never had a visitor, and has never said even one word. When she arrived she was not speaking and we thought that she couldn't speak any more." Now the nurse and I both had tears in our eyes. As I looked away from that woman and toward the nurses' station I realized that all rest of the staff had been watching this wondrous moment, for they too had tears in their eyes.

A few days later, I received an early morning phone call from Janet Savignano, who was our friend and neighbor when we lived in Bolton; she was Amanda's mother. "Amanda," she said, "wants to visit Larry. I am not sure that this is a wise thing for her to do. What if Larry is having a bad day and becomes violent. It would break her heart to see him like that but she insists on doing this. She says that they are friends and he needs to see her. She has read up on Alzheimer's and feels able to go with the flow while visiting. What do you think Phil?"

I took my time answering her. Amanda was now thirteen years old and quite mature for her age. She had inherited much of her father's determination. "This really is something for both of you to decide," I said. "I do think that she understands this illness from what you have told me. If something unforeseen does happen, he usually becomes agitated before an episode. This would give us ample warning for Amanda so she could leave right away." I could not help wondering whether Larry would remember her. It had been such a long time since he had seen her. "Let me know what you decide." I added, "I would want to be there when you come."

The next day Janet called and said that they had decided to visit Larry. She told me which day, and at what time they would be there. I was there on the unit before they arrived. I was relieved to see that Larry was calm. As mother and daughter stepped off the elevator and turned toward me, Larry was looking that way and saw them coming toward him, he held his arms out and said," Oh, Amanda. I am so happy to see you." Amanda ran down the corridor and fell into Larry's arms. "I knew you needed to see me," she said. "You are my best friend. I told my mother that we needed to be together. Do you remember when I was five and you held my hand at my daddy's funeral? You stayed by me all that day. I love you Larry." Amanda arranged herself on Larry's lap. She kissed his cheek and took two of her fingers and stroked his face. "I love you, Larry." She said again.

I was so happy for Amanda, to have been so warmly welcomed by her "best friend." How amazing that Larry remembered her after all those years and how wondrous that his love for her was so enduring.

As each of his friends and family members visited him he would greet them with the same joyous pleasure, always addressing them by their name. If the visitor were one of his children his joy would be even more pronounced.

CHAPTER TEN

Flights Of Angels

"I've come to be with you," I said softly. "This is Phil, do not be anxious Larry dear." I leaned over his bed to stroke his arm. My husband's skin felt so warm; "a fever" the nurse had said, "it often happens this way toward the end". His flesh felt soft, and his hands were limp. "I am here to be with you," I said again, while reaching out to hold his hand.

On this late morning Larry did not return my caress, or respond in any way to acknowledge my presence. The nurse had told me that he was failing rapidly. Now, ironically, I was the one who was becoming fearful. During these recent months I had presumed that I had been the one supporting Larry, yet each time I came to visit him his eyes had focused on my face, and he would glance at me with pleasure, speak my name, obviously delighting in my presence. Suddenly I understood that my husband had always been the one gifting me. Sensations of gratitude and love embraced my soul. His every smile had affirmed the special bond between us; a testament to our hard-carved union of spirits.

Soon my sister, Martha Ann, arrived at the hospital's care center, to share this visit. She had stopped off on her way to spend a few days with me at my home in Woodstock. While my sister sat beside Larry, silently praying for him, I found myself reflecting on the early years of my husband's illness, drifting off into the past. Even then, and all throughout this long and terrible sickness, his loyalty to our special partnership was paramount.

Fifteen years earlier, just weeks before he had been diagnosed with Alzheimer's, we were relaxing together, sitting on the garden bench and admiring our Zen garden. We had created this garden together. Larry had looked at me lovingly and said, "I am so very sorry that I can no longer do the things that I would like to do to help you. I don't understand why this is so; I would help you, if I could Phil". Reaching for my hand he continued, "I hope you realize this."

Now, sitting in his hospital room, I thought back to those times after his diagnosis when I had become silently enraged with him, blaming him in my mind for all our troubles. Rather than facing my own fear I had irrationally placed the complete responsibility for our situation on him. In the early stages of his disease, and because of his efforts to overcome his particular difficulties, we were still able to be active socially, to have fun together, and to take pleasure in the company of our friends. We had traveled, at that time to exotic lands on guided tours. Yet over those years I had not comprehended how much effort it took Larry to compensate for his loss of skills. The amount of discipline these endeavors required confirmed the depth of his love for our children and for me. Looking back at that time, I was embarrassed and ashamed of the way I had responded in my mind to the beginnings of his illness, and to the challenges of his struggle with Alzheimer's.

I felt humbled and grateful for the selfless goal Larry had set for himself in his effort to spare others any anxiety or concern for him. Instead of concentrating on his own problems Larry chose to share with others his delight in the wonders of the world, both extraordinary and simple.

In those days, before we moved to Vermont, he would escort his friends on a tour of our garden in Bolton, often showing them the crimson hibiscus that his very elderly friend, Rita Buckley had given him from her garden. The wild Lady Slippers that grew in the woods on our property also enchanted him. He would walk with us on the soft humus ground, and count these orchid type flowers. "More blooms here this year," he would exclaim, "look, by this tree, two white ones; at last they are multiplying." Watching the birds bring small bits of grass into the birdhouses that he had hung for them on the crabapple trees was, for him, a singular pleasure. He never forgot to put seed into their feeders. At other times he would stand with visitors on our back deck admiring the red-tailed hawks as they circled so high above us only to swoop down to seize a small mouse hiding in the hay field. So many subjects pleased him, and he was happy to share them with others.

He was particularly elated to communicate his happy memories of his youth to each of his beloved grandchildren. It was surprising how Larry now related to his grandchildren. He told them all about his childhood, especially his years in St. Thomas, and how he loved being with his father. These children responded to him in a doting manner. Even four-year-old Amanda, the child who lived next door to us in our winter home, often came to visit Larry. She insisted on driving her new electric car down her long drive, across the unpaved road between our houses, and then up the drive to our house, that sat high on the top of a meadow. She drove, always accompanied by her Dad, happily beeping her horn, to pay a visit to Larry, whom she called, "My best friend."

He enriched numerous others with his openness and warmth and his ability to listen with his heart, and time and again to welcome their affectionate attention. Looking back, at that time years ago it seemed to me that he had been given new proficiencies to compensate for the self-confidence that he had felt when he had the full use of all his powers, and was, in the past been able to resolve the complex challenges he met in his business life.

Before his illness began he had always shared with his family and friends, his unique enthusiasms, and many of the interests that he so passionately held. He was happy to express his thoughts on involvement in, and concern for better methods for teaching at all levels of education. He shared his delight in his favorite classic books, especially "Moby Dick". He would also share his passion for music, in particular, for the brilliant intricacies of the New Orleans jazz musicians. He was a world ahead of me in his appreciation of modern artists such as Kandinsky and Pollock. In those days Larry often instigated many lively discussions on these subjects. He was always more than willing to patiently mentor those who expressed an appreciation for fly-fishing. At times he would talk with zest about the places he had visited in Europe and Asia, or the best restaurants at which to savor the local food while traveling abroad. I had pinned up a super large map of the world on a wall in the kitchen and Larry had placed colored pins on the locations where we had stayed and dined on our travels. There were so many ways he gifted us, enriching our lives and enabling us to discern new kinds of beauty. He had done what the best friendships do, sharing the activities that gave him pleasure so that they soon became our own passions.

As I sat silently beside his bed, on that wintry day, I thought, "It is just possible that I am canonizing my husband in my mind, thinking only of his best qualities and culling out his imperfections."

I was reminded of my aged aunt Marie who once said that she thought it would be fun to be present at her own wake, in order to hear the many accolades of those who would be there. I had rejoined, "Beware of what you wish for; the attendees might not be so generous in their praise."

With a start I realized that my mind was wandering, back and forth into the past. I turned toward my sister Martha Ann, who was sitting next to me, and I said, "We'd best start for home, for this snowstorm is predicted to be a record-breaking March blizzard." She agreed with me that it was time for us to leave. It had been steadily snowing since that morning, and by the time we both arrived back home that afternoon, we could see that this storm was leaving a more than significant amount of snow on the roads. All our way up north we had successfully maneuvered the hills of the highway that were rapidly becoming icy and slippery.

After I arrived at my house, and because the twilight was waning, I let Babette out into our fenced-in back yard. Still wearing my winter parka, with a cup of hot coffee in hand, I stayed outside to monitor her, watching as the little toy poodle explored the hillside, running here and there to follow some scent from a visiting wild animal. I kept an eye on her because the snow was blowing hard now and drifting up and over several parts of the fence that ran around the back of the property. Just a step across and Babette would be free to explore the Village near-by.

"Phil," my sister called to me from inside the kitchen, "it is the hospital on the phone for you." Calling the dog to my side I went into the kitchen to answer the phone.

"I know the weather is terrible," the nurse said, "but we feel that you should come now. Larry has taken a turn for the worse and we think that he is in the process of dying." "I will leave right away. I hope I can make it safely," I responded. I decided that I would have to find a place to stay near to the Hospital, partly because of the weather, and partly because no one knew how long Larry's condition would last. "Perhaps two days," the nurse had mentioned.

I called one of the motels near to the Hospital and was told it had no rooms available; every room was taken due to the storm. "Do you think another motel might have space?" I asked. "No," the woman in charge of reservations replied. "I have already checked availability for another caller." "My husband is dying," I pleaded with her, "my husband is in the hospital down the street from your motel and the nurses feel it is essential for me to be there. All I really need is a bed and a shower. Can you think of anything at all that you might have?" The receptionist then mentioned that she did have a room that had not been renovated and redecorated because it was too small for their new regulations. However, in order to help me out, she said she could send someone in there to make up the bed and clean the bath for me. At least it would be a place for me to hole-up, and to be safely out of this storm. I was relieved and thanked her profusely.

"I'll monitor the phone here while you are gone and watch Babette for you," my sister said, "Don't forget to give me your motel phone number before you leave."

I went upstairs then to search for the suit and the other necessities that the nurse had reminded me to bring for Larry's burial. I threw in a few overnight things for myself as well, putting them into another bag. Once I had packed everything, I said goodbye to Martha Ann, and walked out to my car. As I backed out of the garage I felt relieved that I had thought to fill my gas tank on my way home that day. Once on the highway I patted the dashboard and silently thanked my car for having all-wheel drive which would make all the difference in this storm. It took almost twice the time it usually took to get to Brattleboro for the storm was intensifying. I managed the trip successfully, and without incident.

I decided to go first to the hospital's care center to assess Larry's condition. As I walked into his room I saw him lying on his side with one arm under his pillow and with his legs curled up together. He seemed to be peacefully asleep. I sat on the edge of his bed and I put my arms around his shoulders and leaned over to kiss him. "Larry dear, please do not worry about me or our children." I said, because I wanted to put his mind at ease. I then continued to speak softly to him, "We will be all right dear. If you want to leave your family now, then do so. I will always love you, and I thank you, darling one, for loving me." I could not tell if Larry had heard me or understood what I said to him because he did not open his eyes to look at me, or in any way indicate that he understood me.

The nurse, Clare, came in, and told me that I might want to go and check-in to my motel and rest for a few hours before returning to the hospital, "We will call you if there is any change" she promised. But I decided to spend a little more time with my husband. I walked around my husband's bed, took off my shoes and curled up on the bed beside him. I embraced him and sang to him. I chose to sing "Kindly Shepherd", which was one of his favorite hymns.

When his breathing became more regular I got up to go, kissing Larry softly before I walked down the corridor toward the elevator. Stopping at the desk I left the suitcase with Larry's clothes, my motel phone number along with a list of other pertinent names and telephone numbers for the staff.

I arrived at the motel within five minutes and was shown to my room. I stood by the door and scanned the bedroom. I gasped, "Ghastly!" The colors were all wrong; nothing matched. The motel may have gathered the drapes and the bedspread from the same storage but they did not match. The only chair was covered in purple vinyl with nail heads trimming the sides. The chair could have come from a 1950-ish shoe store, I thought. The room was about ten feet long and eight feet wide. This room screamed to me, "please, help me!" I was immersed in the alien world of paints and patterns planning the redecorating of this little room when the phone rang.

I reached over the bed to answer the telephone, wondering if it was the hospital calling. It was Maureen Gasko, who had stood by me throughout my husband's illness, calling me frequently and sending happy, or humorous cards to cheer me. She asked how Larry was, and how well I was coping with all that was happening. I burst into sobs and tears and began to ramble, "You will not believe what has been going on in my mind. I have been redecorating this room, planning the changes in my head, and all this while my husband is dying down the street from me! There is enough snow here to cover the White House! I made three trips today, one took an hour down to Brattleboro, but it took an hour and a half to return home. Then I had to turn around and do it all over again for the third time and it was much slower and more hazardous than before. I am so exhausted. I can't think properly! I am completely alone, all by myself, in this dingy room. And the nurse said I should take a nap. It would be impossible for me to do that with all that is going on".

Maureen talked to me in a soothing voice, telling me that she was with me in spirit, but would not talk for too long in case the hospital needed to reach me.

"I know that you will be able to handle all that is to come with dignity" Maureen said, "Don't forget that you are stronger than you realize. You will do well. I love you," she added. Calmed somewhat by my friend's kind words, I said, "I know that you are right, I will try to be composed. Thank you for calling me, you are a good friend, but honestly, this is all so boring."

For years to come this last sentence haunted me. Whatever made me feel that way at that moment? My husband was nearby, on his deathbed, breathing his last breaths, and I was complaining that I was bored. "Un-called for"! I would say to myself as I constantly thought about these words in the years to come. And to this day I cannot totally understand this shockingly inappropriate exclamation. Was this train of thought a twisted way of denial, creating a shield for myself in order to avoid facing the reality of Larry's death?

The timing of this call however, was perfect. I was able to put into words the confusion of the day to a friend who called to offer unconditional support. Being able to purge my emotions like this released some of my tensions and I was able to clear my head a bit as I sat waiting for the nurse's call. I had needed a loving and empathetic ear, and Maureen had provided that. As I hung up the phone I realized how important and valuable this type of friendship was to me.

Suddenly all of my emotions shut down and I felt nothing but panic and trepidation. I knew I would need a great deal of strength to get through this night, and perhaps several more days more until Larry died. And then, after he died, I would have all the funeral details to set in place. Soon I would have to face the drive back to the hospital where my husband lay dying. I was desperately trying not to think about the loss of my entire existence as I had experienced it for those many years. I flung myself on the bed, still with my clothes on, trying unsuccessfully to suppress my tears, feeling so forsaken and utterly alone.

A short time later the phone rang again. "Phil, this is Clare calling from the Retreat. I am so sorry to tell you that Larry passed away, just a few minutes ago. It happens like this sometimes. The patients seem to wait until their family has left them; almost as if they want to spare the feelings of the ones they love. And too, this is their time to say their personal goodbyes to all that they have known and loved while they were living and they may not want others to be with them at that time." Clare paused, and then added, "Do come as soon as you can. I will be here when you arrive."

When I stepped off the elevator Clare was there with tears in her eyes. She took my hands in hers and said, "Would you like to see Larry now?"

We walked together down that long corridor to Larry's room. He was lying on his back with the bed-sheet neatly covering his torso. His right arm was across his chest; his other arm was at his side. He looked so serene. His eyes were closed, and his entire body seemed so tranquil. I turned, and realized that Clare had left me alone to say my goodbye in private.

"Goodnight sweet prince," I whispered, "I pray that flights of angels escorted you, as the Good Shepherd carried you in his arms, to bring you to your new home." Then I kissed him gently for the last time.

Now sorrowful thoughts raced through my mind, "He will never again be there to hold me, to touch me, to kiss me or to speak my name." I was filled with grief. I sat beside him on his bed, looking at him for such a long time. At last I said, "Goodbye my love."

As tears spilled down my face my thoughts were racing and skipping around; "Lists, I must make lists," I resolved, as I walked down that long corridor toward the nurses station. I was already thinking of Larry's funeral, which would be the last goodbye for my children.

At the desk Clare told me that she had phoned Phil Callahan to arrange for my husband's body to be brought to Massachusetts. "He wants you to call him now, before you leave," she added.

Phil was more than a compassionate undertaker; he was also a close friend of mine. We had spent many years serving together as board members of an institution that was in a serious crisis. "We are like war buddies," he was wont to say. When he answered my call he explained that he would take care of everything. "There are," he added, "other choices that I know you will want to make. Can you come down tomorrow?" I agreed to come to Massachusetts the next day to tend to these decisions.

While driving north toward my home, I was absolutely determined not to think of anything but the blinding snow all around me, and how to effectively avoid the cars which were skidding out of control on the highway. This objective required every bit of my energy and ability to concentrate. So I drove warily along the road, and finally did manage to arrive safely at home.

As I pulled into my garage I thought, "First a glass of wine, and then I will call my children even though it is very early in the morning now. I am so glad that they went to see their father the day before he died. After I have talked to each of them I shall go up to my room and prepare for bed, and then to sleep; which I prayerfully hope will be a dreamless sleep."

"I'll think about everything else tomorrow;" I resolved, "The plan for my husband's funeral service, the phone calls to family and friends and especially to Larry's best friend, Bob Shea. In the afternoon I will drive down to make all those decisions with Phil Callahan. Yes, tomorrow I will think about all of those things and everything else that I've forgotten to think about today," I resolved, "I will do this when I awaken, after I have had lots and lots of strong black coffee. Later, much later, perhaps many days later, I will think upon this mournful ending to what has been such a painful journey."

As I slipped under the covers of what had been my marital bed, I whispered to myself, "And when shall I think about all that has been lost, and how shall I go on without my friend, my dearest lover? For Larry has left me to go with the Good Shepherd to rest forever in his domain."

"Now I must live all alone. What should I do? When will I be healed of these feelings of desolation? In what ways will I learn to accept this new and much altered life? Into what sort of future will I travel by myself, and for how long, and to where? Finally, at last, I could feel myself drifting off into what I knew would be a restless sleep.

CHAPTER ELEVEN

An Origami Crane

When the autopsy of Larry' brain was complete the Neurologist who had first diagnosed him phoned me and told me that they had found his brain filled with tangles and plaque. He thought, judging by the condition of the brain, that Larry must have been in a coma, lying in a fetal position, for at least six months before his death. But this had been true for only the last two days of his life.

Larry's will was incredibly strong and his intelligence was remarkably high. Was this why he was an exception to the usual progression of the disease? Certainly he was not typical. Did my care make such a difference? Did the care he received at Brattleboro Retreat account for this difference? We will never know. Just as we will never know how much suffering Larry endured throughout his long illness.

After Larry died I found myself reliving the fifteen years of his illness. I was trying to move forward and become involved in the world around me. I could not bring to mind the man I had known before he became ill. I was frustrated from trying to progress in my mourning, I had read Kubler-Ross and understood that these five stages took time. But should it take so very much time?

For several years the memory of my husband's illness haunted me. At first it seemed impossible to let go of those memories. I did not seem able to retrieve images of those happy years before the big "A." I could not place myself there, in the time before his illness, when my loved one was at the fullness of his mind and character. I know that it is natural to suffer from depression after the death of a spouse. Does the mourning for an Alzheimer's patient become unique, last longer, and feel more depressing when the caring takes place over a number of years, causing, at such a snail's pace, the loss of the loved one's ability to function independently, along with the loss of the caregiver's own identity? At that time I felt absolutely estranged from my original self, from the way I had been in the past, full of energy and the excitement for life.

Now my life seemed to have no purpose. My children were grown; my husband was dead. The boards and committees Larry and I had functioned on in years past had forgotten how we had supported them so generously with our time, talent, and treasures. The memory of Larry and the good that he had done in the community had disappeared from people's minds.

I felt adrift. These depressing feelings were lasting much too long. I would have to 'reinvent' myself, find an authentic definition of myself to be my new identity. I had suffered the loss of everything that had defined me in the past, and I felt empty. I needed to search for a new way to live, to restore a tranquil sense of my unique individuality.

Being alone is not the same thing as a sense of absence of self, for I had lost my center. After Larry's death I tried to fill that center with entrainments, such as duties to family and friends and a collection of interests and possessions that did not succeed in helping me develop an authentic definition of "Self". I was creating a cacophony within myself to cover up the real emptiness that was there and falsely declaring this mathematical mix to be a true "Self." This was certainly not a genuine or serene existence.

Yes, I enjoyed my photography, manipulating in Photoshop my favorite images and then printing them at home. I still love this creative process, the ability to generate new beauty. I had a passion for riding and driving and competing with horses, but my financial situation could not support the purchase of new horse, and my health could not sustain the energetic requirements of this sport. Yes I loved reading good books and discussing them at a book club. I had no reason not to continue this passion. I was wearing many different masks in an attempt to avoid living a cohesive interior life. The sum total of all of this striving gave me no stillness within.

Once, when Larry was residing at the Brattleboro Retreat and was completing his first year there I asked him if he still prayed. He answered in the affirmative. Then I asked him for what and for whom he prayed. He answered, "I pray for all those who are here in this institution. They do not want to be here. They would rather be in their own homes. I ask God to be with them and to console them." "Does he console you?" I asked him. "Oh, yes. He is here with me on this corridor. Sometimes he puts his arm around my shoulders when he walks with me." In the midst of his tragic existence, at the end of the fourteenth year of his illness Larry had found tranquility and authenticity.

To achieve this for myself I had to begin an honest assessment of my character.

Facing the reality of one's self is a pain filled process. But I knew that this was necessary. This fragmentation of 'me', this grasping at hobbies to define myself had to cease. I realized that I was looking for a definition of who I was and how I should live in things trivial. This had to end.

I know now that what I had been experiencing is the lot of everyman. Death enters into every life. No one is immune from this affliction. No one is exempt from misfortune. Larry always said that we define ourselves by how we meet life's vicissitudes. I reminisced that even our dog Babette seemed to have a complete understanding of what she was and of her intended role in life. I thought back to an important example of this from the time when we lived in that charming Vermont town. Walking downtown was our morning routine. Larry's career was in merchandising, and, for him, the shop store-windows brought back memories of those years.

One day Larry had asked if he could wait with Babette outside the store while I took a quick peek at the displays inside. When I came out neither Larry nor Babette was waiting for me. It was Déjà Vu time. Should I contact the police first? Should I go home first to see whether, by some freak chance, he might be there? I chose to go home. As I was walking over the bridge that crosses the brook and ends up at the rise that meets our street I looked across the street and I saw him sitting on the porch on one of our wicker chairs with Babette on his lap. My heart stopped pounding I was so relieved.

Once we were all inside the house I unleashed Babette. Just then the phone rang. "This is Ceeley" the caller said. She was my neighbor across the street who had been born in France, was active in the resistance there during the war, and later married an American soldier and came with him to live in Vermont. "I was sitting by my window," Ceeley said, "watching Babette as that tiny dog tugged and pulled Larry across the bridge, up the rise, across our street and onto your porch. I waited, ready to call the police, in case Larry left. But then I saw that Babette had him firmly anchored. Babette knew just how to pull Larry to safety. How that little dog did that I just don't know."

But I knew how she did it. You see she had a purpose, a reason for being. She knew who she was, she knew her importance, and she knew what her job entailed.

After Larry died I felt as though I were cantering in place, like a high-level dressage horse, except in my case, I felt that I was destined to keep this up forever.

I had so many issues to work through. I had lost my identity as caregiver, wife, and my children were married and on there own. My social skills were in poor shape, to put it kindly. I was depressed, a bad sign. I shook my head trying to dispel these thoughts. Then I went to the refrigerator to get a bottle of chilled fruit juice.

This moment was what Reverend Mother would have called "a moment of Grace." Taped to the refrigerator door was the "Gold List." I had begun keeping this list for so many years at the suggestion of my son Larry. He proposed that I begin to keep track of the compassionate and generous actions of others. Those kindhearted gestures, he said, would fill my soul with good feelings and help to balance the troubles of the day. This list would also become a bulwark against self-pity.

I had documented my friends' many considerate acts on this list. There on this list are the numerous notes from my college friends, especially Agnes Van Antwerp, Mary Carol Massaneau and Cathleen Mallaney, all cheering me on! I had noted Peg Andres' and Barbara Lynch's phone calls that brightened my day. All of those considerate deeds, of so many others, were listed there. After Larry died and I had knee replacement surgery my brother Jack and his wife Julie came to lend a hand. Then my sister Martha Ann came to be with me and also to tend my much-neglected garden.

I looked at this long list now with different eyes letting it sink deep into my soul. Now this list of benevolent acts could become an invitation for me to do the same for others who were in need of help and encouragement.

I wanted to find a place where my gifts and my life history could work for the good of others. It seems odd that such a simple thing as a list on my refrigerator would become a catalyst for a momentous decision. That, however, is exactly what happened. I spent the next several days thinking of how I could "gift" my fellow man.

Which of these compassionate gifts was I now meant to emulate? All of them I realized. Whatever crossed the threshold of my life would be the one I must satisfy. It was at this time that I had moved to Massachusetts to be near some of my family. Several years later I began to write this memoir. In the beginning my writings were perhaps bereavement therapy. Then it evolved into a journal of hope, for anyone of us, no matter how seemingly ill suited to the task, with the loving help of the Presence, can mature and grow stronger over the years of coping with a difficult situation.

Now I often look back at those myriad good deeds that had entered my life, and I am grateful to those considerate people who chose to support me and comfort me during those difficult times.

Last year I saw an invitation in the newspaper to become involved in a Hospice program in a nearby institution, Holy Trinity Hospice. As I sipped my coffee I thought, "I have been there, seen and done that, and, as my friend Linda Smith would say, 'I have bought the tee shirt.' I'm decidedly qualified." Was this now the Shepherd's will for me? This ad had jumped out at me! Was I meant now to begin a new journey? Could I face and taste life with determination and a positive attitude, and, especially with humor as my seasoning? I felt that I could. I applied and scheduled an interview. I was determined to be myself in this interview. If the hospice people wanted me for this work it would have to be the real "me". At the end of the interview with David Day he told me that he did want me if the people whom I had named as "recommenders" gave me a good write-up. They apparently did, for I was accepted into the program. Thank you, Monsignor Michael Rose for your kind recommendation. Fr. Mike is an intelligent, empathetic and generous person, and superb public relations for God. And thank you too, Terry Bacharz, for your letter of recommendation. Terry is an extremely organized committee person and is also a lyrical and inspired painter of beautiful works of art.

So I completed the eight-week training course to become a Hospice volunteer. Wherever I go to give solace I shall ask the Presence to go with me. I remember, as David said, that we were all given only one mouth, but however, we were blessed with two ears. Intelligent and compassionate listening will be essential to my role as hospice worker.

When Larry and I were living at the home that had the pond, we had made a Zen meditation garden. It was in a quiet place of natural sand and moss, and various shrubs, surrounded by six giant sugar-maple trees. Now I have a new Zen garden beside my condo. In warm weather I can sit on my lawn chair, next to this garden, and think of Larry, and how he would have loved this new expression of Zen. It is a small garden. The granite Snow-Scene Lantern that Larry and I had bought in Japan is there; it sits by the dry gravel-pond, with a cut leaf dwarf Japanese maple close to it. This garden has all the simplicity and serenity that I now wish for in my life; it is an apt symbol of the 'person' I am now striving to become.

In my library, hanging inside one of my condo windows is an Origami crane. A friend made it for me years ago when I was living in Vermont and taking care of Larry. She made it from a calendar that was illustrated with pictures of angels. "Cranes" she said, "are the messengers of the gods." When I look at it now I recognize it as an emblem of the support that the Presence gives us, perhaps delivered to us by his Angels who are his messengers. That handmade and loving gesture has spoken volumes to me, for this tiny origami cane is a reminder that even the simplest gifts can give great solace to those we love, and may continue to do so for many years to come. This crane itself is a special kind of "Gold List," because it constantly reminds me that I should go and do likewise.

ADDENDUM TO AN ORIGAMI CRANE

I spend Easter, and other times, with my son Larry, and his wife Michelle. Whenever any of their four children are home for a visit, either Elizabeth, Joseph, Katherine or Mary, I treasure having time with each one of them. These grandchildren will always have a very special place in my heart. I feel so wanted, approved and validated whenever I visit this family. Larry and Michelle have been a support system for me over the years.

My daughter Maura has moved to Colorado. I shall miss her. Her daughter Hallie lives there, so even though her son Jamie lives in Georgia, Maura will have family nearby. My esteem for Maura is immense. She has dealt with adversity with dignity, and with faith in her future. She deserves every success and happiness.

My son Eric lives in the next town. He is always available if I need 'brains and muscles'. Eric also takes special care to keep my steak very far from the flames. His wife Jackie is an understanding and thoughtful daughter-in-law. I always enjoy my dinners with them, especially if their daughter Jessica is there.

Martha lives down the road apiece, and it is comforting to know that help is only a few minutes away. Martha has countless friends whom she values. She is always ready to offer her friends support if there is a need. Her two attractive daughters, Madeline and Margaux, are both beautiful in character and a pleasure to be with. Christmas day at their house is so festive. The décor is over the top! My-son-in-law Michael is handsome and witty, and carves the Christmas roast with the proper solemnity.

I am grateful to my Shrewsbury neighbor Lorraine Liskiewicz, who, after yet another of my surgeries, brought my mail to me each day and stayed to chat.

Another kind neighbor, Cindy Day made me the best comfort food when I was recuperating. Her custard is better than the custards of Europe for it is creamy, smooth and delicious! A balm for the soul!

My next-door neighbor, Marion Southworth asked several insightful questions after reading my first draft. I enlarged parts of three chapters in order to present my husband's character in a more comprehensive manner. Many thanks!!!

Roy Hughes, another neighbor, is a photography guru. I have always found that people who really know their subjects are usually the most generous with their time and talent! Thank you Roy!

While preparing my text for the publisher, my neighbor, Bob True, kindly supported me with his extensive knowledge of Word and other types of technologies, all of which I am, sadly quite ignorant. He remained patient and kind throughout the many hours it took for us to complete this task.

My friend Dom Vignola and I have lunch together every so often. Dom is incredibly intelligent, experienced and knowledgeable about the communication industry. He is also a gifted artist. His portraits of animals not only catch the likeness of his subjects, they also portray the personality of each individual animal.

My Gold List celebrates the goodness to be found in so many kindhearted friends.

YES, it is long, because it commemorates extraordinary people. I am indebted to each one of them. I can express my thanks to them by "paying it forward," as my grandchildren would say.

CHAPTER TWELVE

Au Revoir Babette

After my husband Larry died, his little toy French poodle Babette, the dog that had given her complete devotion to him, was eight years old.

For an entire month after my last visit to the care-center where Larry had resided, and where he had died, Babette deliberately avoided me. Clearly, she was in mourning and forlornly disapproved of her master's disappearance. She would not sleep on my bed, or eat anything if I were near enough to observe her. When the doorbell rang she would run to see if Larry had come home, but then, disappointed, she would dejectedly walk away.

Gradually, and at last, she did accept me, first as her alpha, and then as her friend. Now, I had the pleasure of loving a dog that had given her whole heart to my husband. Something good and happy had survived those pain-filled years of a gradual loss of the person I had so loved and admired. Something dear to my husband's heart now filled a significant part of my days with a presence that needed me. Finally, and graciously, Babette gave her heart to me, allowing me to be her mistress. Then she finally accepted me as her companion.

Seven years later, slowly but surely, and too soon, she was becoming a dignified elder dog. Sometimes she could not dance or say her "please". She had all the sad physical problems that very old dogs endure, and now, her epileptic seizures occurred more often and when they did they were more severe. Even going for a walk was something she did now with obvious effort, just to please me. I knew that the time had come to make an appointment with the veterinarian to part with her. However, I kept vacillating, "I will call tomorrow; this is not a really good day to put Babette down," I would think. More and more often I would find her asleep. Even though I knew this was the kindest thing to do for her I still postponed making that call. Why was it so difficult for me to help this failing dog into that last pain free moment? At last, because I loved Babette, I called the vet and mentally prepared for our final goodbye.

When I arrived the vet was waiting, with the appropriate papers for me to sign. I turned to the reception desk, in order to place my signature on them, thus giving my consent to this procedure. Babette and I were then shown into a special room that had a couch and chairs. When our vet returned she sat down on the couch, near enough to pat Babette. Then she said, "I will leave you now to get the medication for Babette, and this will you give you time to say your last goodbye." I sat with Babette in my arms waiting for the doctor to return with the hypodermic. I told her that she had been a perfect dog, helping me with Larry. I kissed her and whispered to her, "For so many years, when your master was ill, you acted as my second in command." I said. "Thank you for your humor and for your consistently happy outlook. You are in my heart" I said, "I will never forget you."

Suddenly this became so much more sorrowful then I had anticipated. Tears were washing down my cheeks, unbidden and unwanted. When the vet returned, she inserted the hypodermic and injected the medication into Babette's veins to spread throughout her entire body. I lifted her close to my face and hugged her gently, saying, "Au Revoir, ma petite, Je t'aime." My lovable, loyal dog seemed to fall quietly asleep, yet, at that moment it felt then as though my heart were being ripped away from me along with a part of my soul. Now I was loosing my last connection to a special being that my husband had, over so many years, so dearly loved.

My sorrow now was equal to the joy Babette had always given to me. She lay in my arms now, so very still. Before I reluctantly handed her to the vet I whispered to her again, "Au Revoir Babette, my sweet one."

That evening I could not sleep. I kept pondering the sadness of that day. "I have put down other dogs and even horses in the past, why has this been so especially traumatic." I wondered. "Why was this such a difficult goodbye, and why do I feel so bereft?"

Lying on my bed, now alone in my home, the realization came gradually, and finally the significance of this difficult day became clear.

"Oh" I suddenly exclaimed. Like a re-run of a family video, a moment from the past came rushing back into my consciousness. The tears came slowly as my thoughts returned to that day at the hospital shortly before my husband Larry had died. It was as though I were traveling back in time. I saw myself there, in that hospital corridor again, standing next to Dr. Rowland at the nurses' station where we were to sign the medical orders that would call for only pain and anti-anxiety medications for my husband. I remembered how it had felt then, on that day at the hospital. It had seemed to me to be so calculating, almost like a betrayal of our mutual love.

In my bedroom, that night, all the pain and guilt that I had felt on that day in the past, returned and washed over my heart, like a rogue wave. That night I could almost feel the Doctor's hand on mine as I had then signed that medical order. "You do not have to do this alone" he had said. I knew in my soul that the medical decision I had made then for my Larry was the correct one and that it had been the loving thing to do because I had not wanted his suffering to be artificially increased or extended. But here in my bedroom, on this evening, I still could not seem to shake those aching feelings of sadness and regret.

At last I comprehended why Babette's final moments were so entwined with those of her master's in my heart. Babette had been Larry's special dog. She had given her whole heart to him, and I had been blessed, and for so many years, to be able to cherish something so dear to my husband's heart. On this day I had lost a being that Larry had loved. With Babette gone the last thing that had been so dear to Larry was no longer beside me.

"I will trust that each day will ease the hurt in my heart and hope that love will enter again, in many other ways to heal me, as it did with my lovable Babette," I thought.

"And I shall always make an effort to remember the days when my loving husband was well and close beside me."

It had been a consolation for me, those years before, to believe that the Good Shepherd had been there beside Larry when he was dying. I had trusted that this gentle Shepherd had gathered my husband's soul in his arms and carried him to his final home with his angels hovering around him. In my mind my thoughts returned to that compassionate Shepherd's Presence in the times when he had been so close to Larry and to me over those Alzheimer's years.

"Dear Shepherd," I prayerfully pleaded on that heartrending night, "Will you graciously allow Babette to be with Larry now? Will you let her dance for him, and perform her tricks for him and say her 'please' so charmingly that she will delight even the Seraphim, and all of your choirs of Angels?" *

*Special thanks to Isaak Dinesen's "Babette's Feast"

CHAPTER THIRTEEN

The Tapestry

We are all travelers in life. Some travel to exotic countries far from home, whereas others travel with their hearts. These are the souls who welcome newcomers to their neighborhood no matter what state or country they come from. These souls have learned to listen with empathy, especially to those who are troubled, offering them the opportunity to articulate their anguish and to take solace in being heard. None of us is exempt from life's tribulations. Some of our days are cloudy, stormy and dark, particularly when suffering enters our lives. Some days are mild and sunny, a time of joy and a welcome respite from everyday troubles.

In photography the shadows enhance volume and create separation of subjects in the image; and occasionally, as in all art, but especially in Caravaggio's paintings, the dark areas enhance the mystery of those areas that are filled with light. Thus light is made more visible for us when surrounded by the presence of darkness.

What qualities in our souls can enrich and increase our ability to appreciate this light and to continue to effectively navigate life's challenges? The most essential are, faith, humility, humor, and love. Assenting with gratitude to faith, humbly recognizing the reality of one's imperfect personality and one's need for succor, cultivating the cathartic release of laughter and opening one's soul to the possibilities of giving and receiving love require great valor when one is walking in the midst of darkness.

"What is love?" I asked my grandmother when I was ten years old.

"You cannot define love," she replied. Then she held out her arms to me. I moved toward her to receive her warm embrace. As she hugged and kissed me she said, "Love, my dear, must be experienced to be understood."

As I matured I began to understand that love is not simply a sensation, but it is a lifestyle made up out of fidelity, concern, consideration, positive action, and desire and determination to do what is best for the one we love. This capacity to love requires courage and wisdom and also the grace to understand when not to intervene.

Love is the original force of that light with which the Creator reveals his Presence. Love is also that which truly validates our souls, for love urges us to reach out in empathy. When one loves a person deeply it is almost a compulsion, this need one has to reach out to minimize his or her suffering, while hoping to mitigate their pain. Love unites us with those who are experiencing affliction, and it is love's compassion that offers to our neighbors the perfect balm.

What then is love? Can it be lost? Is it a sister to those opposing emotions of jealousy, envy and anger? Love requires the absence of those emotions. Love is based on trust, not on fear. How does love continue and prosper? To love well is to see the good in the other, and to desire and encourage that which is best for that person.

Alienation and isolation are frequently the milieu of those of us who live in the "civilized" world today. Often we refrain from touching others, or from generating a true connection with another person. Perhaps we fear the implications of that touch, the sort of obligation that this connection might impose if our touch is returned? Do we hesitate to knock for the fear that the door to the heart of another may never open? And if that door does open, will we then have the courage to enter and discover the goodness that is there? When we are loved well it is impossible to turn away from the complete acceptance, approval and validation that this affirming love bestows upon us. The invitation that this kind of love extends is for us to return this love with joy, to cultivate it carefully, and then in return, to bestow this confirming love on the beloved, always extending it to others close to us.

The accepting love Larry gave to me when he was ill with Alzheimer's generated in me a special kind of anguish, for he trusted me to ease his fears, to reassure him and to heal him. Although I did offer him my loving compassion and comfort, I could do nothing to change his condition. Still, his trust in me continued. He joyfully approved my love despite my inability to prevent his suffering. To be unable to change the course of suffering for the person one loves is the most painful aspect of being a caregiver.

I think that love is a process. The questions not asked create the barriers, preventing love from taking hold in the heart. The semantics of love are not totally dependant on words, but can exist in the simplest acts. Tenderness comes in the reciprocated recognition of all that is loveable in the other. The effects of love are transforming, and yet the unique and all-encompassing "simplicity of love" is a deep mystery.

Humility makes it possible for one to accept the loving generosity of others. If we are aware of our limitations then we are ready to seek and to accept help from others to achieve our goal, with the caveat that we must always remember to pass on this kindness to others.

Humor is the ultimate ingredient that makes it possible for us to survive the darkness by shutting the door against depression and despair. Laughter is the easiest way to gain perspective on life's vicissitudes, enabling us to laugh at ourselves and to return to our daily lives refreshed in spirit. A sense of humor is surely one of mankind's greatest blessings!

With these four, faith, love, humility, and humor, no matter how dark the fear-filled night, we can lift up our eyes and see how brilliantly the stars do shine. We can continue to search out things that are beautiful and actions that are good and rejoice in them. Their existence can be a portent of many providential events to come.

I have long wondered about the reason and purpose for suffering. I have often considered this question over these past years. Why do innocent people suffer? I can see no explanation for it. It is one of life's deepest challenges; a profound mystery. Yet through the sufferings of a woman in labor, a child is born into this world. After surgery the patient suffers, yet that is the time when healing occurs.

Our response to suffering can be the way to unity of spirits, for as the Little Prince said, when you care for someone in need, a bond exists between you and the one you cared for.

Surely Larry must have had moments when he resented his misfortune and wondered why God allowed this tribulation to come into his life. Larry never confided these feelings to me perhaps in an effort to spare me the knowledge of his doubts and his angst as he questioned God's reasoning. In Larry's last year at the Retreat he seemed to have found a special peace, and an acquiescence and acceptance of his fate enabled by the support that the Presence gave him.

We can alleviate the consequences of suffering in the lives of other's in our community. The sufferer and the compassionate neighbor are united in a mysterious way. The suffering of others can elicit the most noble of responses, from the uniquely generous offering of one's organs to another person in desperate need, to the risk of one's life in an attempt to save someone in peril.

Thus suffering can beget empathy, compassion, generosity, kindness, and even acts of extreme heroisms.

What then is death? Is it the greatest of human tragedies? Or is it, like birth, an entrance into a new life? If death was the absolute personal ending of all that was good in a man, including his awareness of himself, then I could see it as the most horrendous event. But if life continues, especially if it is experienced in a higher form, where love and light and joy commingle, then death is not regrettable, it is to be celebrated.

I cannot see how the love that has completely filled a human mind will disintegrate, and cease to exist! For love is the purest act to which man can assent. Is not the love in a person's heart truly the essential reason why he or she will move forward to be consciously united with the Presence? For God is Love, as St. John says in his gospel.

The separation from those we love, and from the lives we have engaged in, must be difficult. To say goodbye to everything that we possess and to each of the beauties of our world is a pain-filled process. To say goodbye to the work of our hands is very difficult and troublesome. The leaving behind of those we love must be the most agonizing of all these partings. It is possible that when a good person dies his or her regrets are partly minimized by the assurance of this departure's being only a temporary separation from all the people whom this soul loved? Does the consoling promise of a new life of unending peace, light and joy ease the separation from the life and the people we have known and loved?

Is it a primary prerequisite that we must consciously chose to let go of our existence in this world, so the gateway to an everlasting renewal of life will be opened to us? At this moment of completed relinquishments do we see the Good Shepherd waiting for us, his hand on the latch of the gate? When he opens the gate for us do we then walk with him into the original light that is Love, and is the definition of the being of the eternal God?

For those who are left behind after a death it is indeed a traumatic loss, for despite the promise of a reunion in the future, this promise is delayed, and the appalling loss in the present must be endured. Then those left behind must have the courage to continue on alone.

One way to reduce the diminishments of another's death is to recognize it as a common cause and to reach out to those who are dying, and to the widows and the orphans who are left behind, giving them a leg up, and offering them our friendship and our help. In doing so we can affect a positive loving balance to all the negatives that death imposes.

At this point in my book, I choose to salute everyone on my "Gold List"; my family, my friends, my college classmates, my neighbors north and south, and all those benevolent others, who have responded to my needs with love and had the courage to reach out to me with empathy. May the Good Shepherd bless you one hundred fold with his kindness and love in return.

I am in admiration of all those who work in care centers, particularly the staff and the volunteers in Hospice.

I choose especially to honor those who work in brain disorder units. Your work is tiring, and challenging, and priceless. You deserve the highest praise for your concern, your patience and your respectful care. You women and men in these vocations are the listening hearts, the compassionate hands, the carefully observant eyes, and, yes, even the voices of the Presence. You do his work. May he hold you in the palm of his hand!

I often return, in my mind, to the thought of the beaches that Larry and I have known, remembering them as they were after a serious storm. These memories have become a metaphor of my life with Larry, for the beauty of nature, especially the sands and the seas, have now become a sign to me of Larry's magnificent character. The horrific storms, however, have become a paradigm of the long years of his valiant suffering during his battle with Alzheimer's.

During those storms, the raging waves throw unique gifts in the flotsam onto the sands. The feathers of the osprey represent to me encouraging messages from the Presence, delivered by his angels. The surfaces of the large damaged conch shells testify to the history of their battle with those powerful waves and shifting sands. These shells wait for us to gently examine them, to lift them up, to understand their unique symbolism, and comprehend their exceptional beauty.

The power of nature is awe-inspiring and inescapable. That nature can be a source of beauty and delight and can inspire poets and painters is one of its greatest gifts. But balancing this beauty is nature's power to destroy. Mankind cannot prevent volcanoes from exploding, or the destructive aftermath. Which scientist can stop an earthquake from happening and sending devastating waves miles across oceans to create mayhem and death? We humans do not have the power to control these forces that are alien to our plans. Neither can any of us predict when, or if, a virulent disease will be discovered in our bodies, or which turn of events will dramatically affect our lives and the happiness of those we love.

Now if the sands shift and wash away from under my feet and I fear that I might sink deeper down until these sands completely cover me, I shall not forget that I am united with the rest of mankind in my fear of the unknown and unexpected. I am now convinced that the Good Shepherd will remain beside me to strengthen me against what ever new trials might come into my life, for he gives me the gift of faith which will overcome my fears.

Is it like this for those who trials are finally over? Do they awaken to a world that is illuminated by a warming light? Is it like the light on the shore after a terrible storm? Do those who have died live in the purity of this newly washed light? Do they find a treasure trove of gifts, gleaming on the silvered sands of this place in which they are now resting?

Why are there such storms in our lives? Is it for what is given to us while these storms rage, or for the gifts we can discover on the beach sands when the storms have ended? With the help of the Presence we can discern these new blessings that have been given to us to console us during our moments of anguish, and to provide comfort after these storms are over. Let us pray that this is so; that we are aware of all his gifts and are grateful for them.

I have a limited time left on this planet in which to perfect myself. However, I am consoled by the fact that I do not know many perfect people. Now I shall cheerfully tread the miles across the sunny green meadows and through the lush forests watching for all things beautiful that lie before me.

Although those woods that I shall walk through "may be dark and deep" I shall sing to celebrate the consolations that have strengthened me in the past. We must always remember that the ways of the Presence are not our ways, and our thoughts are not his thoughts. His plan has a terrible mysterious beauty, and it seems to me, that only by his lovingly holding our hands can we be sustained in the midst of suffering. So I shall sing in celebration of his Presence beside me, even if there will be times when I shall sing as children do, to hide their fear of the dark.

What, then, is the importance of Larry's journey? Why have I been compelled to share it with you? It is because this extraordinary man's life needs telling. Told to you, not just for the way he lived when he was well, but also for the manner in which he conducted himself when he was ill. When he was in control of his mind he always extended his love to all who came into his life. When he was suffering he leaned against the Good Shepherd, who was constantly with him; with his help Larry was able to continue welcoming others with love and enthusiasm.

Larry was a self-effacing person, more concerned with the work to be done than with expected credit for its success. He was always involved in the happiness of the people in his business life, his community and his family.

In the spring of 1983 the Combined Jewish Philanthropies of Greater Boston gave a dinner in Larry's honor. After many kind speeches he was presented with a Vessel that had been excavated in Israel. This object was carbon dated to the time of David, some three thousand years before our time. It is indeed a treasure. The citation on the engraved plaque on its wooden base reads:

> To Lawrence Edward McGourty
> In Recognition for Outstanding Service
> And Dedication to Humanitarian Causes

Larry always considered this tribute to be an exceptional and significant privilege.

Those of us who supported Larry throughout his illness may have helped him to live nobly, which he did, but the uniqueness of his journey was due to his character and his great love for his family and his friends.

To misappropriate Isaiah, "his light broke forth like the dawn." We were privileged to stand in that light

The beach is the place where Larry and I were most aware of the Good Shepherd as he walked beside us. His breath was upon the waters that stretched before us, whispering words of comfort and mercy, "A bruised reed I shall not break, and a dimly burning wick I shall not quench." His presence was felt in the gentlest breeze that caressed our cheeks. We never felt alone or abandoned when we stood upon those sands. In this present moment, as I sit in my studio typing this book, I promise to comprehend that it is my responsibility to appreciate this gift of life that has been given to me. I pledge to try to remember to always reach out to others in friendship, compassion and concern. We too can become the hospitable arms, the voice and the loving empathy of the Presence for those who are strangers, those who are suffering, and, especially for those who are so close to leaving this life and entering his abode. May the Presence grant me the strength, wisdom and generosity to reach outside of myself in order to accomplish this worthy purpose.

I shall now enjoy my strolls across the silvered beaches, the lush green fields and through the autumn woods. Even if I stumble on a rocky trail I shall sing because of the love that enfolds me. I must remember to do this for I have promises to honor. Perhaps singing will help me feel courageous, or conceivably encourage others to join with me in this celebration of all that is good and beautiful. So I shall continue on my journey, singing of the many wonders of this universe, like the Ox Herder, Loa-tsu, sitting atop his water buffalo playing his flute or as the Shaker hymn says, "How can I keep from singing?" My singing will be in celebration of my assurance that I am not alone, and that the path that I am on is the right path. Therefore I shall enthusiastically sing about all the goodness I have experienced, and all the numerous loves I have cherished. Now indeed I must sing, and with enthusiasm, for as my friend, Joan Sweeny says, "God takes to heaven only those who qualify," and, embarrassing as it is, my time has not yet come. Nevertheless the list of my faults is covered up by the list of his blessings. The Good Shepherd knows my imperfections so I am not afraid, for I have seen the evidence of his forgiveness, his mercy, his love, and his generous kindness.

Now the past is gone, and the future is not mine to decide, so I shall concentrate on only those happy memories of my life with Larry, and of all the people whom I loved in the past, and, especially those who now continue to extend their love to me.

I must sing in recognition, and in appreciation for all the goodness that resides in those beside me, for there is so much that is good in my family, my nieces and nephews, my neighbors and in my friends.

I shall pray that Larry's prayer, uttered years ago when he was a patient at the Brattleboro Retreat, will be heard so that all those in brain disorder care centers can know the consolations of the Good Shepherd.

I shall now look with interest to see what new and fascinating events will unfold before me and which ones will engage me and enrich my life. Meanwhile I shall keep on celebrating life, and singing about life, and loving those near and dear to me, and having faith that when my journey here on Earth ends the Good Shepherd will be there beside me, with his hand upon the latch of his gate, to open the gate for me. The joy of laughter will be there, in my new home, for me to share with my husband Larry, and all those other souls whom I have loved.

When the tapestry of our married life is completed the threads that create this fabric shall document the events of our life. The green threads will represent the loving people who have come into our lives, leaving a record of their kindheartedness. The moments of intense suffering will be recorded in the deepest blue. The red threads will be laid down to recall all the loves we have been given and the love we bestowed on others. The yellow threads will be stitched to honor the faith we have been blessed with, the spiritual gifts that we have received, and the doubts that have brought us to our knees. The magenta threads will commemorate our attempts to be humble, while the orange ones will celebrate the humor that saved us from ourselves. Highlighting all our best moments, when we forgave wholeheartedly, and when we gave succor to those in need, will be the threads made from Silver, thick and gleaming. The purest gold threads will be used to outline, in an embracing manner, all the goodness remembered in this tapestry, and the recounting of the authenticity of the Good Shepherd's presence in our lives. These gold threads will document those times when he saved us from harm, guided and supported us, gave us his mercy and forgiveness, and took us in his arms to be with him forever in his abode.

When I am finally there in that abode that is filled with a universal joy, I shall blissfully celebrate with Larry and all those who are there whom I have loved. We shall enthusiastically raise well-chilled glasses to salute all the righteousness that surrounds us.

The Presence of the Good Shepherd will rejoice with us.

Now, at last we see him face to face as he stands there in that space that is filled with his light and his love.

*The Little Prince By Antoine de Saint-Exupery (See Index)

BIBLICAL REFERENCES

From the "Psalter" (See Index)

Ps 16:8   "I am sure God is here, right beside me."

Ps 18:29   "My God, you are my light, a lamp for my darkness."

Ps 22:25   " The lord never scorns the afflicted, never looks away, but hears their cry."

Ps 23   "The Lord is my Shepherd."

Ps 29   "The voice of the Lord is over the waters."

Ps 34:18   "The lord is near to the brokenhearted, And saves the crushed in spirit."

PS 37   "Be still before the Lord, and wait patiently for Him."

Ps 49:1,2,3   "I waited patiently for the Lord he drew me up from the desolate pit.... he put a new song in my mouth."

Ps 69:1,2   "Save me.... for the waters have come up to my neck. I sink in deep mire."

Ps 18   "I will proclaim your might to all those yet Born."

Ps 73:23,24   "You hold my right hand."

Ps 89:22   "My hand strengthens him, my arm encircles him."

Ps 90:4   "In your eyes a thousand years are like a single day."

Ps 90:17   "I deliver all who cling to me, stand by those in trouble."

Ps 95:7   "This is our God, our shepherd, We are the flock led with care."

Ps 103:11,12   "As high as heaven is above earth, So great is God's love for believers.
                  As far as east from west, So God removes our sins."

Ps 105:4   "Look always for the power: For the Presence of God."

Ps 121:1, 2   "I lift up my eyes to the hills beyond.
                  My help comes from the Lord."

Ps 149:1   "Praise the Lord!
                   Sing to him a new song."

Isaiah 41:10   "A bruised reed He will not break,
                   And a dimly burning wick He will not
                   quench."

Isaiah 55:8 ,9   "For my thoughts are not your thoughts,
                   Nor are your ways my ways."

Isaiah 60:5   "The abundance of the sea shall be brought
                   to you."

Isaiah 65:19   "No more shall the sound of weeping be
                   heard, or the cry of distress."

Ezekiel 34:11-16 "I myself will be the shepherd of my sheep.
I will seek the lost, bring back the strayed, bind up the injured,
and strengthen the weak."

Numbers 6:24-26
"The Lord Bless and keep you;
The Lord make His face to shine upon you, And be gracious
to you:
And give you peace."

———————————

John 10:11   "I am the Good Shepherd."

I John I:5   "God is light, and in Him there is no darkness."

I John 4:7   "Beloved, let us love one another, for God is love."

RECOMMENDED BOOKS

"The Psalter"
English translation from the Hebrew
Liturgy Training Publication
Archdiocese of Chicago
1800 N Hermitage Avenue, Chicago, IL 60622-1101

"The 36 Hour Day"
Nancy Mace and Peter Rabins, M.D.
Warner Books Inc
666 Fifth Avenue, New York, N.Y. 10103
1st Edition 1984

"The Loss of Self"
Donna Cohen Ph.D., and.
Carl Eisdorfer PhD, M.D.
Plume (Paperback)
New American Library 1987
(Penguin)

"Alzheimer's- A caregiver's Guide and Sourcebook"
Howard Gruetzner
3rd Edition 2001
John Wiley and Sons, Inc.
(Has Internet Resources
    Video-Movies)

"The little Prince"
Antoine de Saint-Exupery
1971 Harcourt Brace & Company
San Diego California
Translated from the French by Katherine Wood

"Babette's Feast"
Isak Dinesen- Karen Blixen
Anecdotes of Destiny
Publ. 1955
Also
Penguin Mini Modern Classics
Publ. 2011

Alcoholic Anonymous - "The Twelve Steps"

Senior Centers - Pertinent Information- Home Care Information

Alzheimer's Association- Books-Videos-Information

BIOGRAPHY

Phil Gilman McGourty was intimately involved in the care of her husband in their home during the first thirteen years of his long battle with Alzheimer's. He spent the last two years before his death residing in the brain disorder unit at the Brattleboro Retreat in Vermont.

Phil graduated from Manhattanville College in 1949 with a degree in English. She was accepted, in the late sixties, as an independent student in the Philosophy Department at the Graduate School of Boston University to study Asian art, Asian spirituality and Asian philosophy.

Phil has four children, now grown, and nine grandchildren. She lives in Massachusetts. She is a Hospice volunteer, visiting patients at the Holy Trinity Greek Orthodox facility in Worcester MA

For a number of years she wrote a monthly column, "Over The Hill", for the Bolton Common newspaper, under the pen name of "Mini Gilman." In her column, she reflected on images from Massachusetts museums and then wrote a humorous spin on it.

Phil wrote this book because she knows that traumatic times do enter unplanned and unbidden into many lives. She believes that the Power of the Presence of the Good Shepherd can become a support system for the caregiver and the patient. His support will sustain them in their times of tribulation and enable them to courageously, lovingly, and successfully undertake that long and difficult journey.

The Yellow Slickers

Philomene's poignant story of a wife's devoted love in the best of times and through the dark valley of Alzheimer's will touch every reader, especially those who have walked the long road of loving with and caring for a spouse with this degenerative disease. As her husband's illness progressed and he wandered one day from home, Phil remarked that she would never let Larry out of her sight again. This commitment of love would also come to reflect the never ending presence and guidance she would experience from her Good Shepherd.

Reverend Monsignor Michael Rose

Made in the USA
Lexington, KY
10 February 2012